OUR SOUND IS OUR WOUND

Our Sound is Our Wound

Contemplative listening to a noisy world

LUCY WINKETT

continuum

Published by the Continuum International Publishing Group
The Tower Building, 11 York Road, London SE1 7NX
80 Maiden Lane, Suite 704, New York NY 10038

www.continuumbooks.com

First published 2010
Reprinted 2010 (three times)

British Library Cataloguing-in-Publication Data
A catalogue record for this book is available from the British Library.

ISBN 978-0-8264-3921-5

Designed and typeset by Kenneth Burnley, Wirral, Cheshire
Printed and bound in Great Britain by the MPG Books Group

For Mel and Simon

Contents

Foreword

The Archbishop of Canterbury

One of the oddest things about human beings – something that might yet make the sceptical evolutionary biologist pause – is that we make a huge variety of noises that aren't obviously functional. We improvise, decorate, imagine, echo, repeat with variations. The way we produce sound becomes a crucial part of how we find our way around a human world – a world in which other people are making these sounds, sometimes puzzling us, sometimes delighting us.

This is not simply a point about language conventionally understood. It's about all the sounds that bring the world alive in new ways from moment to moment. And as this deeply engaging book observes, the phenomena we are thinking about give an extra dimension to the hallowed biblical truth that creation begins with the uttering of a Word. And this helps us grasp just a little of the still deeper truth, that, eternally prior to creation, God shares, God offers, himself in an eternal act that we can only think of as if it were a great primal utterance being poured out – so that all created things are like echoes of that eternal sound.

'Our sound is our wound': when we engage in the making of sounds we put ourselves at the mercy of others, we become vulnerable in different ways. If we are making perfectly harmonious sounds, if everything is resolved and polished in the sounds we utter or produce, something is wrong, so Lucy Winkett suggests. To be truly engaged in the world as it is requires more than a carefully and beautifully delivered Choral Evensong, however precious this is. There must be ways of connecting with and doing justice to the sounds of the street and of the desert, lament and protest, and sometimes plain cacophony. And we have to listen hard to discern where voices are being reduced to silence by power or violence. Somehow in this process we become tuned in to the most surprising sound of all – the steady plea that God is uttering to us to follow him through the pain of engagement and compassion into resurrection, growing into the heavenly harmony that includes and transforms all our discords.

Lucy writes as a trained singer and musician, and as an exceptionally skilled and sensitive pastor; as someone who is deeply in love with the heritage of the music through which Christians have poured out their devotion to God, but also as someone who hears all the angular and hard sounds of an unreconciled world and isn't content to take refuge in premature harmonies. She has written a beautiful and unusual book, rich in imagery and story, offering real insight into how we set about echoing the Word of God, the eternal self-outpouring that we see embodied in Jesus – in Jesus' speaking and his silence, in his wordless cries and his transforming parables, and in his quiet speaking of our names. Let the reader listen.

+ *Rowan Cantuar:*

Lambeth Palace, Feast of Mary, Martha & Lazarus, 29 July 2009

Introduction

A woman steps onto a stage, her Stradivarius violin tucked under her arm. She glances at the audience as she leads her three companions who carry viola, cello and another violin. The applause that greeted them dies away and the players take their seats in a semi-circle. The violinist lifts her bow. A thousand people are silent: everyone is waiting for the first note. The players have memorized the first lines and so they're looking, not at the music, but at each other. They watch each other, expectant and still, and they wait for the sign that will break this moment of absolute silence – the palpable silent anticipation of sound. Suddenly music begins and the tension is released. The gut-strings are brought to life under the quickening touch of the violinist, and the players are so caught up in the ebb and flow of the music that their feet leave the floor as they rock in their chairs: they lean into one another when the harmony is close, and away when the bowing is full. For the time that they play, they are one. Their unity is costly as they give of themselves to one another, and as together they lay their music before the audience as an offering, a gift they feel compelled to give. The music pours out from and between them, flowing less like water than like blood – a primitive, life-giving gift offered in surrender to the composer's direction and the audience's demand. So vulnerable do they become under the gaze of those watching that their sound itself becomes a wound – a sacrifice that they willingly make, fashioning a beauty that needs neither explanation nor excuse.

The people who listen form a unique company of strangers who have become for one night an audience who experience something unrepeatable. In their minds a hundred questions are raised by this beauty. How did Dvořák know so much truth about life? How does the violin express so much grief in the arms of the woman who plays it? At the end of the concert an elderly man in the audience turns to me with tears running down his face. I can hardly hear his words over the tumultuous ovation as he whispers almost in bewilderment, 'That was the most beautiful thing I've ever heard.'

We live in a noisy world. Has it ever before been this noisy? Lorries, cars and trains thunder through towns and villages, car stereos pump bass-beats out onto the street, background music plays in every shop and restaurant, and the digital revolution means that the volume capacity of radio and television is much higher, causing the manufacturers of new radios to put health warnings on their products to urge their customers to keep the volume down. We measure the depths of the seas with sonar, sending sound to the ocean floor, and, in the skies, the sound barrier itself has been broken. It has been crossed by human beings eager to move as quickly as we can, and we make a colossal noise while we're doing it.

At the beginning of the twenty-first century it became true for the first time in human history that more of the six billion people on the planet lived in cities rather than in the countryside. It is undoubtedly true that in those cities twenty-first-century human beings live in a sound environment unique in the history of humanity. We live in a world of almost constant manufactured noise. It is the suggestion of this book that the sounds we make raise questions not only about how we live and about why we have created the environment we have, but that these soundscapes start to reveal deeper theological questions about who we are, of what we are afraid and in whom we trust.

A key expression of human sound is music. We will be reflecting on this in later chapters, but for now it is enough to say that our relationship to music has changed in one or two fundamental ways. In contrast to previous centuries, our ability to record music makes a live performance in a concert hall audible to many more millions of people than the ones who were physically there. Recording music in a studio means that any mistakes can be removed, and so a technically 'perfect' performance can be produced. It means that music itself becomes a product, bought and sold like anything else. The very notion of beginning and ending music has changed too: the phenomenon of 'repeat to fade', when a pop song repeats over and again the final chorus, has meant that musical endings and harmonic resolutions are no longer obligatory.

Our relationship with music has changed, too, in reaction to the largely hostile soundscape of the city. Thousands of people from every generation (not just the young) create their own soundtrack for life, walking around cities with an iPod, the tell-tale wires hanging down from their ears. Police officers now have a phrase for such people who can't hear traffic coming, or can't hear the bleeping at a pelican crossing. These people, listening to music through earphones, distracted and liable to walk into the road at any time, are 'podestrians', unaware of the effect that they might have on others. We, unlike the vast majority of our forebears, have the capacity to listen to music alone. We are familiar with solitary performers – the folk violinist in the corner of the pub, the piper at the cemetery, the jazz singer spot-lit on a hushed stage. But in previous centuries you would have to be royal-like King Saul asking for David to play for him alone – or extremely rich – to command a performance just for yourself. Now, as a result of recording and downloading, not to mention our iPods, we are able to listen to the Royal Philharmonic Orchestra, or Fifty Cents, or Leona Lewis play and sing just for us.[1] The public aural environments that we share with other people on the street or in a shop or restaurant are full of extraneous noise over which we have little control; but, perhaps in reaction to this, in our private lives we have never had so much power over what we hear.

This book is not so much about hearing sound as about making sound. Of course the two activities are inextricably linked, and in describing the sounds of humanity it is important right at the beginning to acknowledge the varying ability of any of us to hear what sounds are being made. I write as a hearing person who has tinnitus. This will inevitably influence the way in which I write about sound, and it is the tinnitus (in my case, a constant high-pitched whistle) that has arguably heightened my sensitivity to the aural environment, rather than my ability to hear it.

The professional musician Dame Evelyn Glennie is the leading solo percussionist in the world. She lost almost all her physical hearing by the age of twelve, and she uses her extraordinary musical talent to teach audiences, hearing or not, that we experience sound, and therefore music, through our whole bodies. She articulates the difference between hearing and listening. To isolate our ears as the only means by which we can listen to music is, she says, limiting to say the least, and the rhythm of sound and music is felt with our hands, tummies, cheekbones. Our whole bodies are tuned to experience rhythm and vibration and, by becoming sensitive to the intervals between the vibrations, melody too. Her contention is that, with a variety of hearing impairments, we will all experience sound differently, but that we will all experience it somehow. No one who is hearing-impaired should be denied the chance to play music just because those who aren't can't imagine how it happens. It is a failure of imagination rather than a physical impossibility, and the icon of the 'deaf' musician is one that is inspiring, from Beethoven to Glennie to Vikram Seth's pianist Julia, in his novel *An Equal Music*. There is no normative experience against which everything should be measured, and, when we recognize this, our relationship with God and our understanding of human beings will be only expanded and enriched.

In the concert I described at the beginning, I experienced musical sound which seemed to be a wound, in that it embodied vulnerability and personal exposure for the sake of the music itself. This sound was, in the end, a wound that brought a measure of healing, and led the man in the audience to tell a truthful secret to a stranger.

There are clearly sounds that indicate the *infliction* of a wound – a cry of pain when a child falls over, for example – but I am suggesting something slightly different in that the sound itself is a wound and a signifier of something deeper. Perhaps it would be more accurate to say that the sound is an audible scar of damaged tissue underneath; but the sound has substance in itself, in that part of its nature is that of a wound which reveals depth and trauma under the surface.

It is a fundamental part of the Christian revelation of God that Jesus' wounds were visible after his resurrection. Not only were his wounds inflicted publicly, and his crucifixion designed to be seen by crowds, but when he appeared to the disciples in the locked room after his resurrection, he showed them his wounds, and it was in this context that faith was nurtured and peace exchanged.

Wounds are truthful, and their scars link us to our past and provoke the telling of stories. My brother has a scar on his head where he ran into a wall as a small boy. I can still hear myself screaming into the garden for my mother as his face poured with blood. Visible scars from past wounds mark a person out – and, depending on the severity of the wound, that person's identity can become almost wholly defined by one incident in their lives. A woman whose face was burnt in a fire ten years ago walks around the supermarket and knows that the staring customers can tell she has had that experience. It is exposing, as she may rather be known first as a botanist or a grand-mother, but a key and painful experience in her past is revealed to strangers whether she likes it or not.

Emotional or psychological wounds are harder to see and therefore easier to hide. But part of maturing as people, what-ever our circumstances, is that we learn to live with the wounds from our past. It can be precisely from contemplating and accepting those wounds that we begin to mend, and that we learn that it is never too late to start again.

In reflecting on the metaphor of wounds, it's important not to get stuck in a kind of spiritual haemorrhaging. The woman who pushed through the crowd to touch the hem of Jesus' garment was not only deemed unclean but was in danger for her life, and her encounter with Jesus stopped the bleeding, not perpetuated it (Luke 8.43–48). There is a danger as we con-template the crucified Jesus that excessive attention is focused on the wounds both of Christ and of subsequent martyrs, leaving Christians open to the charge of disproportionate morbidity.

Some of the female mystics, for example Catherine of Siena and Teresa of Ávila, developed what was undoubtedly an unhealthy obsession with the blood and wounds of Jesus. This kind of bad religion had led certain medieval women, and sometimes men, to fixate on their own bodies and inflict wounds upon themselves. In a particularly acute case, Mechtild von Hackeborn (1242–99) rolled in glass shards she had put on her bed 'until her whole body dripped with blood so that she could neither sit nor lie down because of the pain'.[2] In contrast to these obsessions, when the Church contemplates Christ crucified, Christians offer modern society the conviction that wounds, which are a part of the human condition, are given meaning by meditating on them in the light of the wounds of God, seen in Jesus. These wounds, inflicted on a human being as a result of fear and cruelty, are indelibly part of the nature of God as the wounded, resurrected Christ returns to heaven.

In terms of the way in which we will speak about sound in the following chapters, it is important to draw a distinction right at the beginning: sound is both actual and also a powerful metaphor. The physical sounds with which we live (including music), some inside our heads, others external to us, will form one aspect of the reflections here. No one knows the fragments of sound that play inside our minds. Some musicologists and psychologists have tried to explore the variety of internal sounds with which we live linked to memory, dreams or emotional extremes, but in the end, no one knows except us. There are also actual sounds that many people hear and try to find vocabulary to describe. We will be thinking about these internal and external soundtracks in Chapters 2 and 3 when reflecting on the themes of lament and freedom.

Sound is also a powerful metaphor for describing our relationship with God. From the description of Creation in Genesis and the beginning of John's Gospel, the action of God has been expressed in sound. Trying to describe the beginning of the earth's life, Jews and Christians have said that God speaks, and Christians offer the metaphor of God as eternal Word. God therefore has a voice, but no one seriously believes that this means God also has a larynx. All language that we use about God is metaphor, in the sense that God is beyond description or language, even though we keep trying to use it. And perhaps because we can't see sound, and God is invisible, the world of sound has proved a rich source of metaphoric descriptions of the presence and activity of God. John of Patmos heard 'a voice like the sound of many waters', Ezekiel heard 'the still, small voice'. We will explore a little of this in Chapters 1, 4 and 5 when we consider the sounds of Scripture, of resurrection and of the angels.

It is an assumption of this book that taking our own contemporary experience seriously is part of the Christian vocation. Jesus of Nazareth used contemporary illustrations and reflections to reveal truths about the nature of humanity and God. In Luke's Gospel he admonishes 'the crowd' by accusing them of not knowing how to interpret the present time (Luke 12.56). Witnesses are those who tell not only of what they see, but of what they experience with all their senses. It is an embodied incarnational theology that helps us listen for the signs of our own times, to try to understand what we reveal about ourselves to one another and to God, and to try to discern the presence of the God of peace as we take account of the cacophony of modern life in a noisy world.

Notes

1. The concept of the 'solitary listener' is explored in Anthony Storr, *Music and the Mind*, HarperCollins, 1993, pp. 108ff.
2. Peter Dinzelbacher, *Christliche Mystik im Abendland*, Paderborn, 1994, p. 231, quoted in Dorothee Soelle, *The Silent Cry*, Augsberg Fortress, 2001, p. 139.

CHAPTER 1

The Sound of Scripture

When I was a child, and heard the Prologue to John's Gospel at midnight on Christmas Eve, I would hear 'In the beginning was the Word', and I would imagine someone – well it wasn't just anyone, it was a big man with a grey beard and a booming voice – shouting 'WORD' to kick-start Creation. In my childish way, I thought that it must at least have needed a yell to do something as serious as create the world. As time progressed, I came to imagine that the word was not spoken at all but sung.

I have realized that many others have imagined this before me. The image of Creation being sung into being is one of the most evocative descriptions in C. S. Lewis's *Chronicles of Narnia*. Aslan sings the Song of Creation in *The Magician's Nephew* and the magical land of Narnia is born. From Australia comes the Aboriginal belief in songlines which crisscross the land, and are tracks of the ancestral songs that sang the mountains and rivers, valleys and deserts into being. It is an aspect of human imagination that has been expressed in different cultures at different times, and is one that generations have found enlivening, as the mythical song evokes themes of melody, harmony and sympathetic participation, helping to define the way in which human beings relate to the natural world. What's more, the authoritative and creative word that comes from the one who made the world then becomes a song that can be taught and learned by repetition and ritual from generation to generation.

For Western societies, as a result of the development of translation and printing, it is the written word rather than the spoken word which has come to carry more authority in public communication. In modern Europe and America, the written word is regarded as more authoritative than the spoken word, which in its turn is more authoritative than the sung word, which in its turn is more desirable than silence. The movement from an oral culture to a written culture has changed our relationship to the spoken word, to oratory and rhetoric, and has latterly included a complex relationship to e-mail as a kind of cross between written and oral communication. When we use either e-mail or instant messaging, we often write as if we are speaking, but the recipient receives a written script, more indelible than our voice. As a result of the election of a poetic and compelling orator as President of the United States in 2008, there are reminders of the power of the spoken word in public life, but in general terms, rhetoric is not as highly valued as it was, say, in the time of Cicero or St Paul; agreements are not binding until they are written, and the verbal offer of a job is less substantial than the compulsory follow-up letter. In the workplace, despite legal assurances about verbal contracts, it is no longer accepted that my word is my bond, and if you don't get it in writing, then that's your problem. We value written words more than spoken words, and that has not always been the case. This cultural privileging elevates literacy and disadvantages those who don't read English well. What's more, it has affected the way we have viewed our holy texts and told our scriptural stories.

The translators of the Bible: Wycliffe, Tyndale, Corvedale and others, are saints of our tradition and are honoured rightly for the skill with which they put the word of God into the hands of the people themselves. But the post-Reformation image of the ordinary man or woman sitting alone reading Scripture is surely both a gift and a sadness. It is a gift in the sense that the power of the literate religious elite, able to control the illiterate congregation, was challenged, but a sadness in that reading Scripture alone replaced hearing it together as somehow the most authentic way to discern the word of God. This may have been an unintended consequence, but *sola Scriptura* ('by Scripture alone'), the doctrine that elevated and detached the authority of Scripture from other types of religious authority, meant also that Scripture in translation was more often read alone.

Only ever reading Scripture alone is analogous to always watching the news alone. It's overwhelming to see pictures from around the globe of cultures and communities that are strange to us, to observe the terrible suffering caused by famine or the movement of tectonic plates under the earth, or stars being born in space. The scope and range of the knowledge we receive from every culture and century mediated to us by the internet or television sometimes paralyses us and we easily develop what has become known as 'compassion fatigue' or 'information overload'. If we share this burden of knowledge with others and discuss what we have seen, it means that we will check out our own reactions. If we dare to let the stories touch us, it's more likely that we will change our behaviour when we've considered what's happening with others. There is both a greater sharing of the burden and a greater account-ability for our actions. Scripture itself was developed by oral tradition in communities, and the primary way in which we can interpret it faithfully is by experiencing it in community ourselves. The text is so rich, and we receive its wisdom through so many cultural and historical filters, our faithful response is nurtured by study in community.

The Bible's production as one book also masks the fact that it is a collection of books written in different languages over centuries. This collection of ancient stories, parables, poems and letters communicates to us the nature, purposes, and above all the love of God. Reading Scripture is not designed to sap our confidence when we are asked to read it out loud to others, but we do often feel anxious about making mistakes. We'll feel less anxious if its sayings, stories and characters get under our skin. It takes courage, for example, but it is vital to talk to children about the stories of the Bible in the same way as they might remember *The Big Friendly Giant* or *The Velveteen Rabbit*: 'Do you remember the bit where he says . . . when she did . . .' and sometimes we might get a detail wrong. As adults, if we know the characters and stories so well that we can simply talk about them as friends, companions and teachers, we will be more able to pass the torch of faith to the next generation without fear.

To honour the origins of Scripture as stories passed down orally among communities, we should take seriously too the interaction between the written word on the page, the author's probable intention, and the contemporary assumptions of the reader. The story of the people of Israel in the Hebrew Bible, the Gospels and the letters of Paul and the apostles, are written for a purpose: to interpret, to persuade, to proclaim. St Paul describes Scripture as 'God-breathed' (2 Timothy 3.16) and that breath gives us speech in order that its Good News may be proclaimed in a sceptical and cynical world. Biblical scholarship helps us here too. Scholars have long developed an understanding of the hermeneutic that is at work when the Bible is read. Whenever Scripture is read, we take into account the relationship between the reader, the author, and the cultures in which the words were written and heard or read. For example, feminist biblical scholars developed a 'hermeneutic of suspicion'[1] challenging Christians to ask questions about the text in order to liberate it from strictly regulated androcentric interpretations, and by doing so, let it touch us more deeply. There are so many wonderful stories in the Gospels that are brought alive by imagining the scene from the woman's point of view and listening for her voice not only of protest against exclusion but hearing too the humour and energy of these first-century women. Listening to the Samaritan woman at the well (John 4), the Syrophoenician woman (Mark 7.24–30), the different aspects of the character of Martha (Luke 10.38–41; John 11.20–27; 39–41) we hear women speak with passion, insight, anger and not a little irony, and it opens our minds, changes our perspective and enriches our experience of God.

I have long found it stimulating to encounter Scripture not so much as a collection of printed words bound together in a volume, but to imagine it in Hebrew, Aramaic, Greek, Latin or English as a soundscape of poems, prophecies, stories and exhortations, laughed over and cried over down the centuries. It's brought to life when it is read out loud, proclaimed, signed, talked about, discussed, listened to, communicated, translated. If we think of Scripture solely as printed words bound in a book, we have tried to capture and flatten it. We even start to believe we can control its meaning, and if we're not careful, forget that its appearance in printed English is recent and not how it has always been. This is not to lessen the importance of close scrutiny and careful study by those who will enlarge our understanding by their attention to detail, but, for the confessional Christian, we can start to feel that this written Bible has the defining status of a dictionary: a book in which we look things up when we have a question. It even has a complex system of reference numbers which increase our accuracy when quoting it, but also increase our anxiety in case we make a mistake. It can become reduced to a book to which we refer in order to categorize and delineate our experience of God.

Scripture (as opposed to a printed Bible) is not conceptually a dictionary-type volume. The translated and printed words have a vital part to play in our experience of and relationship to Scripture, but we can't capture it or flatten it because it is as universal as air and intangible as music. As well as our hallowed book, Scripture is also the God-breathed soundscape of human history in which we listen for the word and the Word to speak and sing.

In 2005, the artist Bruce Nauman created the installation 'Raw Materials' at Tate Modern in London. There was nothing to see. The vast Turbine Hall was empty except for a series of speakers fixed to the walls. As you walked the length of the gallery, you heard voices reciting text or repeating words in varying tones of voice. Because the speakers were directional, you walked through 'walls' of sound before the voice died away and the initiative was taken up by the next voice. Just by the entrance a man's voice repeated 'Thank you thank you thank you thank you thank you.' Further down, another voice repeated 'Work work work work.' Another slightly hysterical voice repeated 'OK OK OK OK OK OK.'

Nauman transformed this cavernous space into a metaphor for the world, which echoes (now) with the endless sound of jokes, poems, pleas, greetings, statements and propositions.[2]

In this installation, sound became a material that was sculpted. The sound 'orchestrated and measured its surroundings'.[3] It was an aural environment that was somehow full even though it was physically empty.

The cadences of Scripture fill the spaces in which we move both inside and outside our church buildings. Like Nauman's installation, Scripture, when read or sung aloud, orchestrates and measures its surroundings. Church services are filled with the dissonance of prophecy, the lament or celebration of the psalms, the harmonies of the Wisdom literature, the conversational tones of the parables, the themes and variations of Paul's letters, and the symphonic apocalypses of Daniel and Revelation. A phrase that accompanies me through Holy Week is one that Sheila Cassidy has used as she portrays human suffering with the haunting sound of sad melody. I in turn imagine listening to the Passion narratives as

... watching someone hollowed out with a knife (with the) end result an instrument on which is played the music of the universe.[4]

By experiencing, reading and listening to Scripture together, as well as reading it alone, we have licence to discuss with vigour and curiosity Jesus' intriguing conversation with Nicodemus under cover of night. We can listen together to the cynical tone of the teacher in Ecclesiastes, the arguments of Samson and Delilah, and the jagged criticism of the religious elite from the young Jeremiah. These stories and sayings have been passed from generation to generation, and in our generation we are asked to lift them off the page where they lie. The canon may be closed but we can't let our minds close along with it.

The difference between reading the Bible and living Scripture is analogous to the performance of music. We can imagine that the written words in the Bible have the function of notes in a musical score. The notes are written down on paper; there is an accepted language of symbols, time signatures and markings, translating the tunes that the composer has heard in his or her head so as to be understood and played by others. But sitting and reading the score of Bach's B minor Mass is an entirely different experience from singing it. The score only becomes music when the players or singers take it up and give it life by playing it. So it is with Scripture.

Evelyn Glennie has spoken compellingly about the relationship between the written score and played music. In her percussion demonstrations, she plays the notes on the page on a snare drum and to the audience it sounds skilful and impressive. Then, she says, she will play 'what is not there'. What she means by that is her own interpretation. The second time she plays the piece, it is recognizable but somehow it comes alive. The difference is astonishing and moving, and her own body language changes as she herself becomes part of the piece the second time round.

In a similar way, words on the page become Scripture when their melodies and rhythms are sculpted before us; when it is read or sung or signed in the voices of the prophets, the crowds, the disciples and the eternal Word – and then lived out in the lives of all who have received it. Scripture makes musicians of all of us, and, just as in the real music world there are sopranos and cellists, conductors and improvisers, rappers and composers, so we will not all play the same instrument or sing the same song. There will be times when we are asked to rest, to be silent, to allow another voice to be heard. But if we don't sing or play the part we have uniquely been given, someone else will miss their cue.

The literal music of the Bible provides the foundation for our exploration of these themes. Biblical scholars have tried to reconstruct the Hebrew chant patterns used in the Temple at the time of Jesus. It is well for us to remember as we attend church services during which there will always be a reading from the Bible, that in first-century Palestine, all of Scripture was a song. The French organist and musicologist Suzanne Haik Vantoura spent four years attempting to decipher small notation marks made above and below the Hebrew script in the earliest manuscripts of the Old Testament. While it is impossible to say with complete certainty that this is how Jesus would have heard Scripture, her research has found acknowledgement in Temple studies groups, and her reconstructions of the Hebrew Scriptures have been recorded.[5] We may be familiar with the psalms as songs, but it is a remarkable thing to listen to the prophecies of Isaiah or the Creation narratives in Genesis sung in this way. I have experienced it when it was sung by a Jewish scholar and found myself transfixed by the rise and fall of the chant. I found myself picturing Jesus in the synagogue at Nazareth unrolling the scroll and not so much declaiming as singing that the Spirit of the Lord was upon him, and that in his mission to comfort those who mourned he would proclaim the year of the Lord's favour (Luke 4.16–21). In listening to the reconstructed Hebrew chant, I realized that this prophecy is a beautiful song, and the singer no less a figure than Adonai, the troubadour Lord, singing a love song for his suffering people.

Some years ago I took part in a recording of Thomas Tallis's motet *Spem in Alium*. It is a piece written for forty voices, all singing a different part. Forty singers stood in a circle with the conductor and, in eight groups of five, we rehearsed and sang the motet together. It is immensely complex, and, while listening hard to other voices in order to keep time and relate what you are doing to the others, it is also important that you sing the part you have been given. There are bars' rest too – where each singer must remain silent to give room for other melodies to be heard. The changing dynamics of the ensemble and the intimate communication necessary between the singers make the sound somehow luminous, even though technically you could analyse the indications on the score and explain why it got louder or brighter when it did. And as many times as it is rehearsed, it is never quite the same twice. To record the music meant simply to capture one time that we sang it – a mixture of obedience and interpretation enlivened by the unique dynamic of that particular group of singers. The recording can then be shared with others who weren't there and who, by listening to it, can experience the music with a degree of immediacy that means they feel as if they were. Recording the music also means that it is somehow commod-ified – it becomes a thing that one person can buy or give or receive. The CD is a physical product which gives a wide audi-ence access to an essentially small event. The written score, the inspiration of the composer, the physical presence of the singers, the recording of the sounds and the production of the CD are all stages in the music's mission. *Spem in Alium* is a demanding piece, and it is an intense piece that can take your breath away, especially when all 40 singers sing together for the first time. Because of its 40 different parts, the physical scores of music are huge, and Tallis' achievement is all the more impressive as he would not have ever seen it all written out himself. It was composed by him from the sounds he must have heard within him, and was only later transcribed for singers to see all the parts together. Probably written in the mid-sixteenth century to celebrate either the birthday of

Queen Mary or Queen Elizabeth I, it is a song of humility whose depth can't be expressed either by knowing its historical origins or by simply looking at the page:

> I have never put my hope in any other but in you
> God of Israel
> who will be angry
> and yet become again gracious
> and who forgives all the sins of suffering humanity.
> Lord God
> Creator of Heaven and Earth
> look upon our lowliness.

The context of its composition is hardly rooted in spiritual revelation – it had a more political birth, celebrating the life of the monarch – but its spiritual power and theological assurance become evident when it is sung. It is music from a past century, sung by contemporary singers, that can inspire us to live more hopefully in the future. In this way, its significance transcends time and it demonstrates the resurrection of the dead, in that Tallis's voice is heard years after he has fallen silent. It also gives us a model for human community as the communication between singers, composer and conductor enables the sound to rise and fall and every voice to be heard. It is music that evokes commitment, assurance, wholeness and sincerity of purpose.

Most people, if they hear such live choral music at all, would experience something of this sculpting of a Scriptural sound-world not in a church but in a concert hall, perhaps in a performance of a confessional piece like Verdi's *Requiem* or Elgar's *The Apostles*. They might also experience short bursts of it as 'lift music' – the so-called muzac that constitutes the background noise of shopping centres, advertising features and helplines when we're put on hold. But I have often marvelled at a packed-out Albert Hall (over 5,000 people) listening to church music in secular surroundings – for example, a Renaissance Mass setting which, to my ears, is incomplete without the Eucharistic Prayer. There is a thirst for this music, but its live performance belongs now more often in the concert hall rather than in the working church. Audiences are not all grey-haired either. Young people in jeans and tee-shirts fill concert halls and listen to music by Tomas Luis de Victoria or John Taverner. Cathedrals and churches which do have the resources to sing this music in its liturgical context continue to do so not only as a commitment to high-quality music but theologically, as a statement of ecumenism (Roman Catholic Mass settings are often juxtaposed with anthems and hymns by Methodists in a typical Anglican choral Eucharist) and as an affirmation of the God who, incarnate, transcends the centuries. When one visits Hampton Court or the Tower of London, one sees a reconstruction of a life and culture that is no longer active. When one hears the music of William Byrd in a living act of worship, one is simply witnessing the latest generation of people who will pray through it. It is living heritage: the contemporary edge of a long tradition that is still evolving and moving forwards.

When I try to listen for the profound and varied sounds of Scripture, they are nowhere more evocatively expressed than in the music of J. S. Bach. Although G. F. Handel is more revered in Britain, with local annual performances of *Messiah* still being sung around the country, Bach's contribution to Western imagination and spirituality is immense. His is a sound-world that in its scale and depth accompanies us on a profound spiritual and musical journey. The bass notes travel, often at walking pace, rising and falling, journeying through the narrative with delicacy but with seemingly inexorable harmonic confidence. The melody is horizontal, often based on Lutheran psalm chants or hymn tunes, pointing us always forward in the direction of travel. The harmony is vertical, but again travelling forwards, moving us on, resolving, moving us on again, taking us through the sadness of minor keys to the brightness of the major. In the horizontal melody and the vertical harmony, I can hear, as others have before me, Bach's cross-shaped faith that brings meaning in a chaotic world. I find the music consoling and emotional, and, in its journey towards musical resolution, I learn that the movement of the Spirit is to bring order out of chaos. In the movement and energy of the harmonies, it seems too that reformation is always possible, that things do not have to be as they are. Although the music is not afraid of turbulence, in the spirit of Psalm 107 it travels with us through the storms of our lives to the haven where we would be (Psalm 107.29–30).

Bach's music also has an air of anticipation: even if you are not familiar with the musical form of theme exposition, development and recapitulation and so on, you can feel that somehow a question has been asked, and, as you listen, you find yourself waiting for something. You know that something familiar is going to come back soon, but you don't know how or when or in which key. Bach's music bears much analysis, but the analysis will not tell me in the end why I am consoled by it, why it comforts me, why it tells back to me the story of the sorrow of my soul.

Bach was inspired by his own faith to write such music, but it's not only within the Church or within liturgy that Scriptural cadences are heard. The continuing nature of revelation means that in contemporary popular and classical music our own generations hear the rhythms and sounds of Scripture – sometimes unacknowledged, sometimes explicit.

Ms Dynamite – her real name is Naomi McLean Daley – grew up in north London and has won awards on both sides of the Atlantic for her politically aware blend of British hip hop, R & B with catchy choruses. She explores issues such as gun crime, domestic violence, women's rights, and, in her last album *Judgement Days*, asked pointed questions of her listeners:

> What are you gonna do when he comes for you?
> Where you gonna hide when he comes for you?
> And when he questions you,
> I wonder what you're gonna say on judgement day?[6]

Ms Dynamite describes herself as an atheist, but it is possible to detect resonances of Matthew's Gospel and the picture of Christ dividing the sheep from the goats (Matthew 25.31) in her lyrics. The straightforward, even confrontational style of her questions finds resonance with Matthew's stark emphasis on the eschaton (when one woman will be grinding flour and one will be taken: Matthew 24.41). Ms Dynamite is more concerned with now rather than then, and is highlighting the reality of judgement to galvanize her listeners to act well in the present: a realized eschatology. Her wandering melodies and irregular beat do not make for easy listening, but the pulse is seductive and her strong lyrics demand change from political leaders and are an energetic protest against the inequalities in society. She sings from a context where her advocacy of fundamental change is born out of her own experience. For her, and for people she knows, life is not acceptable as it is. Ms Dynamite performs not only at her own gigs, but also at political events such as 'Love Music, Hate Racism' in memory of Anthony Walker, the eighteen-year-old who was killed in a racist attack on Merseyside in the summer of 2005. She is a musician who makes connections between her musical expression and her life in the world. She uses the medium of music to tell the truth.

Another artist in the UK in whom Scriptural cadences are detectable is the Birmingham-born Mike Skinner from The Streets. He has also inspired many others who have imitated his laid-back style. He talks as well as sings his music and has a conversational, even chatty rap style over repetitive drum beats and simple chord progressions. Often the choruses are sung by what sounds like a crowd of friends. It is not slick, and is designed to sound as ordinary as a bloke in his room talking about his day. But the themes are not just the personal ones of finding or losing a girlfriend, although romantic love makes an appearance on his albums. He sings with wit and inventiveness about the ecological crisis, history, ethics, faith and doubt. He uses metaphors and stories from everyday life to explore themes of blessing, evil, love, materialism and human vulnerability to despair. He is interested in big questions of right and wrong, and finds accessible, funny ways of expressing these themes. On his last album (the lyrics of which he describes on his blog as an inner monologue) he explores the desirability of going to heaven (where the weather would be better) or hell (where he would prefer the company). He imagines a conversation with the devil, and, in common with many before him, decides heaven would be boring. But he also resists the temptation to sign up to the devil's contract. Underneath the unglamorous packaging and simple tunes, he is addressing the serious questions of life with contemporary illustrations. He has been described as a storyteller, and he himself has said that he wants to express meaning in his music.[7] His censure of organized religion is vociferous, and, along with many artists, he articulates a strong critique of any religious elite who try to prescribe what is right and wrong. But he is a poet who is using the vernacular to express universal themes, and as such sings truthful and hopeful songs that inherit the techniques of the parables.

Let us be clear what we are saying here. Neither Ms Dynamite nor Mike Skinner would accept being claimed by a religious institution, and both have been sharply critical of organized religion. But as artists they are not afraid to engage with the deep questions of trust, hope and the ethics of modern society. Even while they offer a thoughtful critique of religion, the cadences and rhythms of Scripture are audible in their song.

They express these deeper themes in contrast to much of the popular music of any genre that provides the soundtrack to our high streets. Most of the time, we are listening to a version of New York City or LA culture that looks alternative but is in fact thoroughly corporate. Music videos shown on 24-hour cable channels illustrate songs with the predominant themes of crime and personal relationships. Impossibly thin midriffs have virtual sex with an invisible partner – all for the voyeur and helped by the low waistlines currently in fashion. The search for power, money and no-strings sex provides the narratives for these aspirational videos where teens and twenty-somethings congregate, often by a large swimming pool in the sun.[8] Even while male singers sing of women as bitches and casual violence is part of daily life, it seems that women have the power of humiliation; the men's fear of being belittled revealed by their permanent clutching of their crotch throughout the song.

The music that is sung and played in church has to be heard with this wider perspective in mind. It is a good discipline to ask ourselves within church communities where our sounds sit in relation to the music so widely broadcast in society. When the Church comments publicly about modern music and culture – or even when we attempt to make a distinction between sacred and secular music – we can't avoid the place the Church has within culture. Choral Evensong has become, as Tim Gorringe has commented, an 'artefact of high culture':[9] it is claimed not only as an expression of Christian faith but as an object on display when a certain kind of Englishness is being described. It doesn't help that when we in the Church attempt to connect with 'modern music', we tend not to mean really modern music: we generally mean The Carpenters.

The Church is bound to proclaim two truths revealed in Scripture: that God is both transcendent and immanent; beyond us and beside us. The sounds of this Scriptural revelation resonate nowhere better than in music. Music expresses the 'otherness' of God – the exuberance of God expressed in Haydn's *Nelson Mass*; the mystery of God expressed in Messiaen's *O Sacrum Convivium*; the sadness of God expressed in the *Good Friday Reproaches* by Vittoria or Sanders; and the freedom of God expressed in *Oh Happy Day*. It is somehow over us, bringing the eternal into the present and transcending our earthbound existence. Music may supremely express the transcendent, but it also embodies the immanent. In the creation of music, there is often a patron, a struggle, a political and financial context in which the composer works and the performers perform. The theological language of grace and gift is the language of faith; but lurking underneath the gift of music, the free exchange of sonant beauty, is the language of the market, of contract, of obligation and commission.

We have already mentioned the development in reading Scripture alone rather than hearing it together as part of the process of translation into the vernacular. In musical terms, the group experience of the sounds of Scripture were beneficial to congregations unfamiliar with Latin. The Reformation called into existence a body of religious music that eventually favoured the vernacular although anthems were written in English and Latin. Great English composers Christopher Tye, Thomas Tallis, John Sheppard and Robert White wrote in the last blossoming of Latin motets. Tallis's pupil, the Catholic William Byrd, composed in Latin and English. At this time, the sound-worlds of Church and street were not too far from each other. Byrd's anthem *In Laudibus Sanctis* is full of cross-rhythms and wild syncopation that would have delighted contemporary secular madrigal singers arguably more than the sober singers of plainchant. Interestingly, like modern popular music writers, Byrd's politics were not far from his music; the rich chords and emphasis on the word '*Verum*' in his motet *Ave Verum Corpus* revealed Byrd making a musically substantive point about transubstantiation.

But the movement in language from Latin to English texts was not so much a matter of church politics as of generation. Tallis and Byrd wrote in both Latin and English, but Byrd's pupil Tomkins, along with Thomas Weelkes and Orlando Gibbons, wrote entirely in English.[10] The famous *Western Wynde Masses*, written using a secular song accompanying eucharistic texts, were popularized first by John Taverner and then by Christopher Tye and John Sheppard. The Wesley brothers of the eighteenth century and Vaughan Williams in the nineteenth and early twentieth centuries brought into liturgy familiar tunes from the villages. It is ironic that such hymn tunes as 'Kingsfold', 'Monk's Gate' and 'King's Lynn' are now regarded as highbrow or inaccessible when their origins are popular and nothing of the sort. It is one of the most often repeated criticisms of people attending church that they can't join in the hymns. The timeless power of the folksong with a strong tune can carry across the generations when they are taught well, which won't stop us looking for new, good tunes at a pitch that is comfortable to sing.

There is little connection in modern urban contexts between the sound-world of the Church and the sound-world of the street. Inside a church building, you are more likely to recognize the sounds of Radio 3, Classic FM and a simplified version of Radio 2 than Radio 1, Jazz or Kiss FM. This is an unusual thing in the churches' history to be so culturally specific and arguably detached from the majority experience. There is more recognizable connection with popular culture in the style of music played by a worship band, but it is still mostly of a genre that is reminiscent of late 1970s early 1980s soft rock. It is unchallenging musically, although often uplifting and enjoyable. A good worship band can lead a congregation in praise like few other accompaniments and can move congregations to tears with well-tried harmonies also used in secular love songs. Someone once commented to me from a congregation that he was puzzled by what he called 'tribal' attitudes towards music in the Church. When a particular type of music accompanies a party line, and its style becomes one of the criteria by which a church community is judged, then the music itself is in danger of becoming an idol. Church communities are singing gospel music, experimenting with jazz vespers and reggae beats, but the truth is that most churches in Britain are making musical sounds that in cultural terms would be classed either classical or easy listening. Arts Festivals such as Greenbelt and Spring Harvest go a long way to showing that music with a Christian theme can be skiffle, jazz, punk or hip hop, but these remain by and large special events with gigging musicians. With notable exceptions, the stereotype of church services – either older people singing hymns or younger people singing choruses – remains.

In claiming the right to comment critically and imaginatively on the cultures in which it is embedded, Christians sometimes adopt an oppositional stance, but this can leave us on a cultural island on which we build our religion and our case. Our music as well as our theology can become too self-referential, taking our cultural reference points from a narrow set of 'acceptable' places. The split in music between 'high' and 'low' culture is regrettable; it can certainly set the Church up in a judgemental position, as not only a guardian of high-skill musical performance but as a rather snooty arbiter of taste. I recently heard an academic musicologist say that broadcasting Choral Evensong had done for church music what Barbie had done for women: that is, offer a perfected standard that ordinary people find hard to emulate, inducing guilt and anxiety when they can't. It was a sharp point and drew an intake of breath from the audience, but as a cathedral precentor I felt somewhat convicted, as the speaker went on to identify that a false sense of competition causes unnecessary anxiety and discontent, when parish Evensong with one or two people in the choir doesn't sound like it does on Radio 3.

As a lover of Choral Evensong I want to affirm that the combination of Cranmer's Prayer Book emphasis on the Incarnation, together with the transcendent sound of choristers in an evocative acoustic, is a compelling combination for an exhausted urban population looking for peace. The conversational rhythm of the versicles and responses, the ancient wisdom of the psalms, the prophetic energy of the *Magnificat* and the sure touch of Simeon's *Nunc Dimittis* faith, together with anthems that may be from before the Norman Conquest or written especially for that service; all these elements create a sacred space filled with the sounds of Scripture within which can be held that day's events, disappointments, disasters and delights. Prayer Book Evensong is a precious gift that deserves our commitment and our love.

But equally, as a lover of Choral Evensong, I want to say that it is important we do not ignore its underside too. We can't leave unexamined the self-confessed 'addiction' to Evensong that is sometimes expressed. It can foster an undeniably pedantic spirit in us, and, in allowing that pedantry free reign, our spirits, instead of soaring in praise of God, can become earthbound in defence of the past. And while the sixteenth and seventeenth polyphony of which we are so rightly proud makes a vast contribution to the enlivening of the canticles, there is a developed precision about it which takes us to the edge of a spiritual cliff too. A concern for excellence can lead to intolerance of human frailty; a respect for the musical genius of the past can turn into reluctance to commission young composers encountering the sacred texts for the first time; the invitation to the congregation to come and rest and not have anything asked of you can turn into exclusion of the very people the Prayer Book was constructed to reach.

Moving from the sound-world of the street to the sound-world of the Church can be an arduous journey which few make because they mean to, and most make by accident.

The urban sound-world that many people occupy is hostile, as we shall explore in later chapters. Because the sounds that we live with are monotone, relentless, with occasional bursts of warning or control, we lose our connection with our inner world. More and more of us choose to block out the physical sound-world with which we are surrounded and buy an iPod where we listen to a soundtrack we have chosen. There won't be much that isn't familiar to us, all mistakes are airbrushed out, and we control the content and volume of our own private recital.

When we gather for worship, for example at Choral Evensong, there will be mistakes in the music; we will be asked to stand and sit with others; we may even be asked to sing. The live musicians will inspire or distract us and a relationship develops across time and space with the composer (perhaps long since dead), the performers and the congregation. This develops in us a completely different relationship to the music from the one we have to downloaded or recorded tunes. We are not in control: the variation in volume will be huge compared with what we are used to; and unless you are in a large cathedral, with thousands of organ pipes, it is likely to be much quieter than you would hear through headphones. There will be endings and silence too: there is no endless 'repeat to fade'. Experiencing live and unamplified music sometimes makes people laugh or feel embarrassed. It is another way in which Christian worship has become disconnected from other, more regular experiences of sound. In St Paul's Cathedral, where up to 500 people will attend Evensong every day during the summer, and never fewer than 80 in the winter, many can't really believe what they are seeing and hearing. Despite our confidence and belief in what we are doing, it is sometimes a little difficult to resist the feeling that we are in some kind of ecclesiastical branch of the Sealed Knot Society re-enacting events from the seventeenth century for our own enjoyment.

Whatever many of the people who come think of what they hear, there is a power in the tried-and-tested liturgy of Evensong. The sounds of Scripture are disturbing and healing, and music is one of the best ways for these theological themes to be taught, shared and proclaimed. But we cannot claim that this is an exclusive prerogative of the Church. If Christians are prepared to be culturally inclusive, we won't express that just by singing religious songs from around the world (although that's important too), but we will listen, really listen, to the tone, cadence and content of modern popular music and initiate dialogue. Instead of damaging ourselves with tribal arguments about which music is appropriate or proper, as often happens in our communities, we can nurture within ourselves a spirit of cultural curiosity. We could borrow from a library or buy online a CD of a type of music we have never heard, just to see what we can learn. We could choose a CD of music that we suspect we won't like, in the spirit of non-violent resistance to the apathy that persuades us that we know what we like and we like what we know. Our interdependence as human beings and as Christians includes our music. There are voices both inside and outside church communities that move us, that teach us about love and touch us. I am glad I heard Freddie Mercury sing live before he died. The guts with which he sang 'Who Wants to Live for Ever?' stays with me as an example of the strength of the human spirit in adversity. Recordings of Maria Callas, Billie Holiday, Jesse Norman, Frank Sinatra, and, in our own generation, voices such as Amy Winehouse, Pete Doherty, Joss Stone, are all special. Christian communities, wherever they are set, can continue to play their historic role of patron of the arts and music and find ways to encourage young and old people to sing.

When we listen for the sounds of Scripture, we can hear that the centuries of experience related within it encompass the whole range of human emotions. We also know that the sounds that society is making in reaction to the story of humanity are evolving. The question is, do we evolve along with it? Never before has the range of music played in society been so diverse. The classical music world reacted to the world wars of the twentieth century in the clashing chords of Stravinsky and Schoenberg. Music in church, strongly influenced in the first centuries by Greek ideas of harmony and the music of the spheres, retains a reluctance to admit dissonance into worship. Plato argued in *The Republic* that disharmony was akin to evil speaking. The Pythagorean and Boethean theories of the music of the spheres linked harmony with the calm, circular motion of the planets, as God intended them to be. These ideas heavily influenced Augustine and the early Church fathers as they struggled to find a place for music in Christian worship.

But when we listen to our own contemporary sound-world in the Church, we might recognize that, if we may put it like this, after Auschwitz, it is not appropriate that before God every cadence resolves, or that every rhythm is comforting. We must allow for dissonance in our worship, for the expression of human experience such as that articulated by Ms Dynamite and Mike Skinner to be authentic in the presence of God. There are classical composers who write for the Church such as Judith Bingham, Judith Weir, Gabriel Jackson, Francis Grier and others who are writing music that is not afraid to be dissonant. But we have not moved fundamentally from the idea that harmony is good and disharmony is bad in music, as it was argued by Aristotle, Augustine and Aquinas. Resolution and harmony is not always the sound we hear in Scripture, which tells the story of God who willingly became subject to human violence and whose wounds were still visible after he was raised. Disharmony is evident too in the lives of men, women and children across the world whose dignity is stripped away by poverty, war, oppression and disease.

In the Church, our sound is our wound when we ignore the dissonance in this aching world; of unemployment, debt, poverty and abuse. Our harmony is not real harmony if it is bland resolution that trivializes the singer and the song. It is a harmony that is made when we listen to the dissonances of Scripture and experience and deepen our understanding of another. It is the harmony that is made when we listen for the voice that is singing a different part, even one that sounds contrary to the part we are singing. It is a harmony born of an attentiveness to God and to each other that means we will listen and take our rest as well as play and sing the part we have been given. This is the harmony that takes account of the suffering of God's broken world, and as we listen for that profound song of love, we can invite others to sing.

Notes

1. Elisabeth Schüssler Fiorenza, *Bread Not Stone*, Beacon Press, 1995.
2. Emma Dexter, curator, Tate Modern exhibition catalogue, 2005.
3. Dexter, Tate Modern exhibition catalogue.
4. Sheila Cassidy, *Good Friday People*, Darton, Longman & Todd, 1991, p. 5.
5. Suzanne Haik Vantoura, *The Music of the Bible Revealed*, Bibal Press, 1991.
6. Title track from *Judgement Days*, Polydor, 2005.
7. www.skinnermike.com.
8. See Benjamin Barber, *Jihad vs McWorld*, Random House, 1995, pp. 100ff.
9. Tim Gorringe, *Furthering Humanity*, Ashgate, 2004, chapter 3, pp. 47ff.
10. *The Concise Oxford Dictionary of Music*, Oxford University Press, 1985, p. 261.

CHAPTER 2

The Sound of Lament

I visited a friend in hospital. She is in her early forties, and has been living a full life while managing a serious degenerative physical condition which has required her to use a wheelchair for all of her adult life. After suffering a stroke, she had been resuscitated by doctors who weren't sure enough of her wishes to let her go. As a result, she had very little control over the movement of any part of her body; she couldn't speak clearly, or eat or drink; she couldn't tolerate light, or touch – even from her husband – but she remained acutely alert in her thoughts and emotions. As I pushed open the ward door to find her bed, I heard a terrible sound, which was something like a shriek, somehow more lacerating than a scream. A sound of rapier – pure anguish. An overwhelming sound that I have not heard before or since from a human being. A sound of fury, regret, despair and violent refusal to accept the present moment. I didn't want to believe that this sound was coming from my friend. I hoped it was another patient, one whom I didn't know and would not have to face, and my heart pounded and my eyes pricked as I rounded the corner and saw what I didn't want to see – that it was her. The sound made me want to put my hands over my ears and cry for her to stop. Like an animal afraid to draw near to a fire in the forest, I circled the bed, feeling the heat of her pain and knowing that I would be burned by it too.

The sound of lament is heard throughout Scripture. It is more than a cry of grief, more than a purely human reaction to a distressing event or oppressive situation. It is both a protest against the pain of the present time, and also a timeless expression of the weeping voice of God, in whose image and likeness we are made. It is contemporary because, in the midst of lament, all that exists is the searing pain of the moment. It is also eternal, in that our tears join the lament already begun before the ages by the blood of Abel crying for vengeance from beyond the grave. Human beings cry for the loss of life, for the loss of a future, for the loss of hope. In its power and precision, our personal lament lacerates the stodgy platitudes of well-meaning friends and expresses the paradox that in the midst of life we know we are in death.

It's in the prophecy of Jeremiah that we hear the lament of Rachel echoing down the centuries weeping for her children:

> Thus says the LORD: a voice is heard in Ramah, lamentation and bitter weeping. Rachel is weeping for her children; she refuses to be comforted for her children, because they are no more. (Jeremiah 31.15)

In his inspirational commentary on Jeremiah, Walter Brueggemann comments

> The sound comes out of the ancient past; Mother Rachel grieves over the generations, for all the lost children who are so vulnerable and so brutalized. Mother Rachel is disconsolate for all the lost children of Israel, including the current generation of exiles. The weeping of the uncomforted mother easily traverses the generations, for all the lost ones are the same to this mother, regardless of their generation.[1]

Brueggemann shows that because of the force of the Hebrew verbs used in these verses, the prophet is expressing the huge power of the very act of vocal remembering. At the sound of Rachel's lament, God 'utterly remembers' and then 'utterly has mercy'.[2] There is a quality of uncompromising absoluteness about the act of lament and God's response. Lament is visceral, not mannered, and it makes itself heard without our permission or initiative. Although later formalized in liturgy, in origin lament is involuntary, as if we were retching out our pain.

Jeremiah tells us of Rachel, the uncomforted mother who weeps for her lost children. I, too, have seen the uncomforted mother who refuses help into the car at her daughter's funeral. The uncomforted mother who dares not accept the sympathy cards because if she opens them and reads them and puts them on the shelf, it will mean that Stephanie really has died. The uncomforted mother whose open eyes at 2 a.m. see nothing but the ambulance door closing, separating her from the one to whom she gave birth. The stubborn, resolute, defiant, uncomforted mother, who will not be patronized or touched, who will not think it her duty to make anyone else feel more at ease, who will probably kill with her bare hands anyone who asks her how she feels. 'I will not cease from mental fight', she sings, knowing that, even in years to come, this will be true.

In modern times, this lament has been heard from Darfur to Beslan, Srebrenica to Sri Lanka. The uncomforted mothers were heard on the afternoon of 12 May 2008 when at 2.30 p.m. the most powerful earthquake in 32 years hit Sichuan province in China. It was just the time when schools, orphanages, factories and hospitals were full. As the shoddily built school buildings collapsed, unimaginable grief poured out as mothers and fathers, restricted to a single son or daughter by the government's one-child policy, lost all their family in that young life.

I heard the sound of lament in Trafalgar Square during the Israeli government's bombing of Gaza in January 2009. Thousands of people gathered to protest, to be together: young and old, Arabic-speaking and English. Al Jezeera television played on large screens, broadcasting the tablar and violins which wailed their accompaniment to the pictures of more uncomforted mothers lamenting 300 children killed in 22 days. At the beginning, the crowd itself was quiet, with gently swirling flags, buckets being shaken with an understated, tentative 'Please contribute to the cost of the demonstration.' Into the relative calm, a loud, high-pitched shout from the young woman at the front, whose voice was made tinny and thin by the distorting microphone, led the crowd in chants and songs expressing the lament of a people in anger and grief.

An artist told me in conversation that he had visited a convent and talked with one of the sisters there about what Mary, mother of Jesus, would have done on the evening of Good Friday. They imagined together that she would have gone to visit the mother of Judas. He painted this scene: two women, two uncomforted mothers, sitting talking together about their terrible, terrible day.[3] The imagined scene of these two mothers sitting together after the death of their sons was reminiscent of another meeting, this time not of grieving but of expectant mothers years before – the visit of a younger Mary to her cousin Elizabeth. If Elizabeth had lived to see her own son John the Baptist executed, the three would have had much to share on that first Good Friday: the uncomforted mothers of sons at the heart of the story of salvation.

Echoes of these conversations were heard in July 2005 after

the bombs had exploded on the Underground and on the bus in central London. Not only victims' relatives were interviewed, but the mother of one of the bombers was asked to comment by a journalist. It was reminiscent of that imaginary meeting between Mary and the mother of Judas. She said in a television interview:

> I do not know how to grieve for my son. Instead I will grieve for the victims, for the dead and injured.

In her voice, numb with grief and bewilderment, it was plain that the sound of suffering does not come only from the mothers of the innocent.

In Scripture, the tradition of lament in the mouth of the mother is set alongside the other iconic image of lament: that of the song of the daughter. We first meet the lamenting daughter in the eleventh chapter of Judges. Jephthah is about to go into battle against the Ammonites. He makes a vow to God that if he is granted victory, then:

> Whoever comes out of the doors of my house to meet me . . . shall be the Lord's to be offered up by me as a burnt-offering.

Jephthah thus vows to sacrifice the first creature he sees on his return. He fights the Ammonites and is victorious:

> Now Jephthah came to Mizpah to his home. Just at that moment, his daughter came forth to meet him with timbrels and dances. She was his one and only child; besides her he had neither son nor daughter. Upon seeing her he rent his clothes.

Jephthah tells his daughter the vow he made to God and also that he, although his spirits are very low, will keep this vow. She asks for a period of two months to lament with her female friends in the wilderness and to prepare herself for death. At the end of this time, we read simply:

> . . . she returned to her father and he did to her his vow which he had vowed.

It is, as the Hebrew scholar Phyllis Trible has named it, a Text of Terror[4] – an abusive and unjust act that is precipitated by Jephthah's daughter's song, first of rejoicing and then of lament.

Her first song is that of joy. She dances and sings, unaware that her action seals her fate. She is in the tradition of Miriam, who:

> . . . took a timbrel in her hand and all the women went out after her with music and dancing. (Exodus 15.19–21)

Years later, when David returned victorious from battle with the Philistines, we hear:

> . . . the women came out of all the cities of Israel, singing and dancing, to meet King Saul, with timbrels, with songs of joy, and instruments of music. And the women sang to one another as they made merry. (1 Samuel 18.6–7)

As a consequence of performing her traditional duty in song, Jephthah's daughter is condemned, because she was the first creature that her father saw. It is a desperate end to the story. The vow made by Jephthah, intending to bargain with Yahweh and secure victory for himself, results in the death by fire of his only daughter – at his own hand. Into the voice of this daughter is placed the celebration of an army's victory, which in turn leads to her lament for her own shortened life. What's more, it doesn't end there, as we hear that remembering her own lament in the wilderness became an annual tradition in Israel. She became the nameless voice of a nation (Judges 11.39–40).[5]

The sound of personal lament is ancient and timeless, from the uncomforted mothers to the weeping daughters to the despairing fathers. And an individual lament can become the lightning conductor for the grief of a generation. In the second book of Samuel, King David's son Absalom is killed in battle, and the lament of David over his son has been given haunting melody by the fifteenth-century French composer Josquin des Prez in his lament *Absalon Fili Mi*. The grief of King David over his son has inspired some of the finest music of the Tudor period, including Thomas Weelkes (1576–1623) in his plaintive *When David heard that Absalom was slain*. For other composers of this period, for example Weelkes' pupil Thomas Tomkins, their best and most richly harmonic music is saved for their settings of this particular text. The repetition of 'My son, my son' gives powerful musical expression to poignant and profound heartache. Writing in a time of high infant mortality, these fifteenth- and sixteenth-century composers express something of their own generation's grief by telling the story of David's. Scriptural lament reaches across the centuries even further with this particular story too. In the biblical account, Absalom is set upon by a mob and killed, a chilling description of a lynching, even down to the detail of his being hanged in a tree.

In 1937, a Jewish schoolteacher in new York, Abel Meeropol (he is better known by his pseudonym Lewis Allen), saw a photograph of the lynchings of Thomas Shipp and Abram Smith.

He said at the time that it was this photograph that haunted him and inspired him to write the poem 'Strange Fruit'. He showed the poem to the jazz singer Billie Holiday and they worked on the music together. Its bitter imagery describes the strange fruit hanging in the poplar trees: the hanging of a black man by a white mob. Because her own record company wouldn't let her record it, Holiday found an independent company which released it, and it became a hit, reaching Number 1 in the United States of America in July 1939. *Time* magazine originally described it as 'a prime piece of musical propaganda', but in 1999 it was voted the song of the twentieth century.

> Southern trees bear a strange fruit,
> Blood on the leaves and blood at the root,
> Black body swinging in the Southern breeze,
> Strange fruit hanging from the poplar trees.
>
> Pastoral scene of the gallant South,
> The bulging eyes and the twisted mouth,
> Scent of magnolia sweet and fresh,
> And the sudden smell of burning flesh.
>
> Here is a fruit for the crows to pluck,
> For the rain to gather, for the wind to suck,
> For the sun to rot, for a tree to drop,
> Here is a strange and bitter crop.

Billie Holiday sang this powerful and disturbing lament in many different contexts, and she herself told the story that one night in a club in Los Angeles she was asked by a woman to sing what she called the 'sexy song you're so famous for – you know, the one about the naked bodies in the trees'.[6] She refused to sing it after such a gross misinterpretation of what the song is about. It is a song once heard, never forgotten, and although it is sung by one voice, it expresses the lament of a whole people protesting against the wickedness and sadism of which human beings are capable. When she sang it at the Apollo Theatre for the first time, the owner Frank Schiffman said that after her performance there was 'a moment of oppressively heavy silence . . . and then a kind of rustling sound I had never heard before. It was the sound of almost two thousand (black) people sighing.'[7] It sings out its indictment across the generations of a complicit society's silence faced with the cruelty of the mob. By the time Billie Holiday released her record in 1939, public awareness of the practice of lynching was growing, but this song became hugely influential, not only in raising awareness of racism, but also in inspiring solidarity and activism in campaigning against it.

The song highlighted the previously hidden story that, before emancipation, thousands had been lynched, and many went unrecorded. In some cases, the crowds that gathered to watch were very large, and, of the tens of thousands of lynchers and onlookers, a handful were indicted. White families brought children to watch, newspapers sometimes carried notices of upcoming lynchings, family excursion tickets were sold, and postcards were sent to family members recording the events. There's a postcard depicting the lynching of Lige Daniels, Center, Texas, USA, 3 August 1920. The back reads, 'He killed Earl's grandma. She was Florence's mother. Give this to Bud. From Aunt Myrtle'. Many similar postcards were made as souvenirs. There was often a carnival atmosphere. Collective fantasies are perpetuated by communications such as this. The twenty-first-century equivalent of that early twentieth-century postcard are the video-sharing sites where the sounds and sights of the totally inappropriately named 'happy slapping' are available to all viewers. This modern form of lynching is a feature of city life where a person is attacked and sometimes killed for being black or gay or white or whichever category of humanity is despised by the attackers. The 'post-card' is written by the recording of the violence on a mobile phone. The laments of King David, of Billie Holiday and Abel Meeropol are echoed in the protests against the violence of our cities today.

Lament seems to have been a feature particularly of city life as early as the second millennium BCE. The tradition of public lament was recorded over ruined cities and temples in southern Mesopotamia as part of Sumerian culture. It was in this tradition of urban lament that Jerusalem became the subject of the book of Lamentations after the destruction of the Temple in 587 BC. The destruction of the Temple was a catastrophic event for the people of Israel and precipitated a definitive tradition of lament that may well have become part of the ritual of the urban population. In Joshua 7.5–9 we read of special days set aside for lamentation, which was accompanied by fasting, wearing of sackcloth, weeping, rending of garments, putting of dust and ashes on the head (for example Judith 4.9–15). Lament was a vocal expression of grief in reaction to the forces of destruction: a natural disaster or a war.[8]

> How lonely sits the city
> That once was full of people!
> How like a widow she has become,
> She that was great among the nations!
> She that was a princess among the provinces
> Has become a vassal. (Lamentations 1.1)

Lament as a formal expression of grief in the face of death survives in folk traditions all over the world, where the chanting, instrumental music and singing of dirges is normally carried out by women (sometimes relatives of the dead and sometimes, still, professional lamenters). In modern urban culture, however, the place of lament is all but lost, though it is still the case that, in times of war and at moments of destruction or natural disaster, days of official mourning are called and national memorial services are held. In Italy, Good Friday 2009 was a day of mourning for those killed in the L'Aquila earthquake, and Australia held a national day of mourning for those who died in the bush fires earlier in the same year. In the UK since the beginning of the century, national laments have taken the form of televised church services remembering those killed after 9/11, in the war in Iraq, in the tsunami disaster of late 2004, and by the 2005 London bombs.

As we shall discuss in a later chapter, the fact of death is much less acknowledged publicly than in previous generations, and rituals of public mourning – the laying out of the body, the wearing of special clothes, the gathering of extended family – have for most people now translated into three days' compassionate leave from work, and attendance at a quiet funeral. In British cities like London, Birmingham and Liverpool, where people from many cultures live, public mourning is still visible and audible from time to time, and the more recent practice of leaving flowers at the site of a death has provided a way to mark tragedy in the public realm, but collective national mourning after death has been formalized to the lying-in-state of public figures.

In listening for the sound of urban lament today, it is not so much our reaction to physical human death that I want to discuss, as the qualities and characteristics of a society's lament in the face of deathly habits and structures. If an individual lament is to some extent involuntary, visceral, a signifier of pain in vocal expression, then in a society where the tradition of formal, communal, intentional lament has been lost, perhaps lament takes the form of an involuntary expression of pain faced with the prospect of nothingness.

While formal intentional lament is in decline, listening to the city reveals a variety of involuntary, visceral lamenting sounds in reaction to forces of destruction that caused the development of lament in earlier times. The forces of death, so opposed by Jesus, are still here: selfishness, greed, fear, violence – the inexorable drag into nothingness that can bedevil our life in the world if we loosen our hold on all that we believe is good and beautiful and true.

A modern urban soundscape is characterized by the qualities of relentlessness and monotone. I used to live in east London on a busy highway into the city. The only times I witnessed the road fall silent was Christmas Day. The low, insistent drone of cars, vans and buses was constant throughout the day and night and was punctuated by the sirens of police cars or fire engines and the beep-beep warning every few seconds of the zebra crossing just outside the church community centre where I lived. The road on which I lived in Handsworth in Birmingham was similar, with the monotone more often broken by the rhythmic thump of drum and bass spilling out from a passing car that was loud enough to resonate in my chest while I sat in my flat. The volume and content of these spikes of noise are culturally conditioned: it's much more likely to be Dizzee Rascal or Eminem played at high volume on the high street than it is Joni Mitchell or Vivaldi. The soundscapes with which we are surrounded are out of our control, both in content and volume. Busy streets, such as Oxford Street in central London or Green Street in east London or Brixton High Street in south London, where the combination of traffic, music from cars and shops, together with the talking of thousands of people on the pavement, mean that we shout into our phones or to our companions as we move slowly forward. Noisy cities are not new: in the early nineteenth century, the poet Shelley likened the sound of London he heard from three miles away to the sound of a swelling sea. The metal wheels of carriages on cobbles were deafening and mixed with the shouts of market traders and the sounds of horses and dogs. Noisy but arguably more human: the development of mechanization and amplification have made the sounds of the twenty-first century unique. Even buskers and street musicians almost all have microphones and speakers to make themselves heard above the traffic.

Away from the sounds of the street, we are surrounded by the manufactured sound environments we find when we enter shops, bars and restaurants and the huge shopping centres in which we can easily spend days shopping and eating without seeing the sky. The bigger department clothes stores have their own radio stations with playlists to suit the type of customers they hope will buy the clothes. Thought has been given to the music they play, and the leakage of sound out of the door will often be in inverse proportion to the cost of the goods inside. In broad terms, loud indicates youth and inexpensive, quiet indicates wealth and 'class'. We go about our everyday business largely unaware of this background sound, and we rarely reflect on what we are experiencing, just as we will not often examine wallpaper in the bathroom. It's just normal life, but noting the sounds we hear, and what effect this has on us, bears reflection and a little analysis. A short, regular trip to have a haircut reveals one type of manufactured sound environment when we stop to listen.

I walk into the hairdresser – and the music, pulsating fast, is loud. As I walk through the door, the young male singer is singing about having sex with a woman he has recently met. It's just loud enough for everyone to have to raise their voice slightly and has the effect of making you think you have arrived at a party. There is intimate touch here, from the young woman who washes my hair to the man who cuts it – and who reassures me in murmured professional tones that the grey is 'not really that visible'. The aural environment creates a fantasy of youth, of social interaction with glamorous strangers, with a hint of danger and flirtatiousness. What is actually happening is quite functional: a row of standing people are, with scissors, cutting off the hair on the heads of another row of people who are sitting down. For most of the time, my hair is wet, plastered to the side of my scalp, and I look straight ahead at the mirror in front of me, invariably thinking, 'Blimey, she looks tired.' After the functional haircutting is over, there is an economic transaction at the till with some low-level beeping and some exchange of pleasantries (normally 'Thank you' several times) to cover the reality of money changing hands. Yet I invariably walk out of the hairdresser feeling better about myself than when I went in. The fantasy sound-world has done its job. I feel somehow a little lighter and that more is possible.

This particular manufactured sound environment is designed to sell haircuts and colour treatments. Presumably, the theory is that creating the fantasy of a party will increase the confidence of the customers and make them feel as if they have joined a group of glamorous people younger than themselves. While they undergo what is actually a fairly practical procedure, they experience, if only for one hour, the atmosphere of a kind of safe club. It is designed to encourage repeat visits – that is, sell more haircuts – and so the music is chosen with their target clientele in mind. In a fast-food restaurant, the lighting is harsh and the music slightly annoying in the hope that customers will do what it says on the tin: eat fast and leave their table for someone else. The environment is not designed to make us linger. We are not aware on a day-to-day basis of the choices that others have made as they surround us with sound. The sounds of these artificial environments reveal the city's wound of relentless commercialism. We are surrounded by inducements to buy, which make people, in all their varieties, into homogeneous customers, categorized by their ability to pay.

Although our experience of everyday sound is largely unacknowledged, we are consciously aware of the power of sound in some ways. One of the most heavily criticized developments of 2008 was the placing of a device called Mosquito which emitted a high-pitched tone only heard by people under 25. The device was designed to dissuade large groups of people under 25 from congregating outside shops and supermarkets. A campaign run by young people (appropriately called Buzz Off!) attacked the use of this device, and as a result of the protest, a number of companies and councils reduced its use. As a method of maintaining public order it has its supporters, who say that it works. But as an articulation of how a civilized society regards its young people, it is an indictment of the adults. This sound is the wound of a society that seems to despise and fear its young: there is arguably no other group of people in society against whom this would be tolerated. The decisions we make about sound reveal our attitudes, and the campaigning involvement of the civil liberties group Liberty is a reflection on the fact that the right to freedom from unwanted noise is fast becoming part of the legal framework of the state.

In the sounds of the street – those that no one has co-ordinated or controlled – there are natural sounds that are masked by the all-enveloping noise. Foxes are there, but are not often heard except in the tipping over of rubbish bins; birds are sometimes heard, but their song is different; the wind that blows through the leaves of the trees is audible only in the centre of a park, but not on the road; and there is no silence. The soundscape of the countryside and the city are self-evidently different, and, while there are clearly unpleasant sounds in a rural context – for example the slaughtering of pigs or the shooting of a horse – and there are pleasant sounds in the city – the excited chatter of friends in a bar, or the laughter of skateboarders having fun – the city soundscape nonetheless is full of repetitious and monotonous noise which threatens our connection with the music of the natural world.

There is something poignant about the song of birds in the city. I live near to the River Thames, and seagulls cry each morning. When I wake up, I can feel for a moment that I am by the sea. Memories of childhood holidays – snippets of memory and half-remembered conversations, the smell of salt, the taste of ice cream – are triggered by those seagulls, and somehow I take my childish innocence into Morning Prayer as well as the more surface concerns of today's meetings and e-mails. The sound of birdsong is a sound that has inspired composers, artists and poets throughout the centuries. Because scientists tell us that bird bone structure and behaviour are close to dinosaurs, they are somehow, for me, the indigenous people of the skies; the descendants of pterodactyls, the survivors of the ages. And the interaction between birds and their urban environment reveals one aspect of the lament we are listening for.

Birds sing to find a mate, to mark out territory, to warn other birds of danger. They sing in spring, they sing as dawn breaks, and their song marks the passing of time and seasons. But recent research has shown that birds sing differently in cities. While their ability to adapt to their environment is impressive, changes in their song are also a warning to us. Like the canary in the mine, their sacrifice warns us of danger we can't see. In cities, birds are singing not just in the daytime but at night, in reaction not only to light pollution, but to noise too. A series of articles in the *New Scientist* magazine explored the findings of researchers at Leiden University in the Netherlands, who found that birds were singing songs more quickly and at a higher pitch than in the nearby forests. Hans Slabbekoom[10] found that in ten European cities, birds were singing faster and higher than their counterparts in forests close to those cities. Their theory is that because traffic noise tends to be at a low frequency, birds hoping to attract a mate will sing at higher frequencies to be heard. In forests, however, the variety of frequencies is maintained. Professor Richard Fuller from Sheffield University found in 2005 that robins were singing at night in places where noise pollution during the day was at its highest.[11]

Another study has shown that urban birds are singing more loudly too. Nightingales were recorded in Berlin in 2001 and 2002 singing at 95 decibels, as loud as the New York subway. This necessity to sing so loudly may damage their lung function or may send the evolutionary process in a new direction; none of these consequences is clear after such a short time of study, but they are undoubtedly singing more loudly as a result of the city noise around them.

Scientists continue to work on these studies, helping us understand the witness of the birds as they show us what effect our choices have, not only on us but on the creatures with whom we share them. What seems to be happening is that birds are singing more loudly, at a higher shrill pitch, with less variation and in the dark in order to make themselves heard over the human noise of low-pitched, monotonous, relentless sound. Night has become the new day; the urban world is inside out.

Despite the decreasing variation in melody and higher pitch of the song, I still imagine the robin or nightingale continuing to sing over the drone of traffic as the aural equivalent of plants breaking through a pavement. The solid monotone of humans transporting themselves from here to there and back again doesn't seem to be able to suppress the melodic creativity of a blackbird, even if his singing has to become more piercing and shrill. It is still a hopeful song, tragic and wistful but historic and full of ancient wisdom.

We have begun to use the language of the natural environment to describe our aural surroundings. We now speak of 'noise pollution' and we know that if it is sustained sound 24 hours a day it is a contributing factor to high stress levels and even illness. The World Health Organization has begun investigating the effects of chronic noise exposure and has found a percentage of deaths from heart disease can be attributed to long-term stress caused by noise. The UK Office for National Statistics discovered in May 2007 that noise complaints to government offices have increased fivefold over the last twenty years.[12] We are quite literally annoying one another to death, as a large number of these complaints are against noisy neighbours.

The business of leisure generates its own sound-world too.

Apart from the noise emanating from bars and restaurants, our desire for even more television channels means that tarmac, that sits like a thick layer of black icing on top of the earth, is dug into to lay more and more cables to more and more individual homes. City roads are dug up several times a year, all by different private companies, puncturing the utilities' infrastructure beneath our feet. The desire of vast numbers of people to spend their leisure time surrounded by loud music while consuming high levels of alcohol is a clear strain on those who live around pubs and clubs, and so it seems we are entertaining ourselves into an early grave too. It's important to say that the all-enveloping sound of loud music in a club or a pub is great fun, and to dance to it is a great pleasure; but when I do it, I also recognize in myself that I'm enjoying a sense of escape, rather than finding any lasting satisfaction.

What does this constant noise reveal about ourselves? On an individual basis, not much. The wall of sound that emanates from city-centre pubs for example will be made up of a thousand different individual voices: the laughter of friends at a long-planned birthday party; the last-minute agreement to meet for a drink after work; the pint or two to delay an arrival home; the hysterical shrieking of a hen night or a group of lads 'on the pull'. Listening to each individual voice will reveal that everyone is there for a different reason, and hardly any of those reasons would be classed as a cause for lament. But as a collective wall of sound, it strikes a high-pitched note of energetic, anxious laughter: the competitive storytelling of colleagues trying to keep up; the over-eager downing of the first drink just 'to take the edge off'. In volume and pitch, the city-centre pub culture reveals a mixture of need and aggression that gives the sound of the crowd a poignancy more eloquent than the feelings of any individual. It's poignant because it's the sound of a society reassuring itself that we do not have to be alone, that the money we have is ours and we earned it, and that we should enjoy ourselves now because we are afraid of what will happen when we die.

But before we demonize the individuals who are so vocal on a Friday and Saturday night outside the bars and clubs of our city centres, or the workers who shout at each other in the bars of city financial districts, it is important to say that these are our collective sounds and they are the wounds of a whole society. In identifying this neediness and urge for escapism, we are not listening for the bleating sound of the goat sent off into the wilderness to atone for the sins of the people. There is no virtue or purpose in blaming one sector of society for what 'they' do. In this sense, although society is certainly economically and socially unequal, before God there is no 'them and us', there is only 'us'. It looks like fun but is driven by fear. It seems to be unthinking, a deathly routine designed to bring comfort in a demanding world. We are all part of the collective maintenance of values in our society that put almost intolerable pressure on individuals to succeed personally, financially and socially, the pressure that is temporarily relieved by the dash to the pub at 6 p.m. or the sustained excesses of the weekend.

Similarly, we are all part of the collective maintenance of values that mean 'more and faster' is self-evidently better than 'less and slower'. While very few would publicly defend assessing the value of human life in purely economic terms, our collective behaviour sometimes betrays our unacknowledged motives: maximum gain for minimum effort, and a search for self-worth in the therapy of retail. Stories of shopping crowds stampeding and in some cases trampling each other or shop staff appal us, but we don't find it all that surprising. Despite every world religion attempting to teach its followers to value what has no price, the fact is that even in the midst of the global downturn, not many people that I spoke to who worked in financial services predicted a truly fundamental shift in the values on which our competitive economic system is based or in the methods by which those values are maintained. Many, if they kept their jobs, predicted a medium-term reduction in economic activity, a chastened financial sector simply lending and trading less, followed by some kind of slightly pared-down business as usual.

The point is that in what sociologists are calling late modernity, our urban sound environment expresses something of our values and desires, and, I am suggesting, of our wounds too. In a market economy, reliant on trade, delivering products more quickly than competitors has increased the volume of traffic (in both senses of the word). In a society that equates privacy with status, the majority of cars take only one person to work. The greater your disposable income, the more privacy you can buy and the less time you have to wait for anything, including your transport. While the poor or elderly queue at a bus stop, the rich have a car waiting outside the meeting. Our capacity to do more, to generate more, to spend more, is a symbol of our power, and so speed is valued to the extent that journeys are a nuisance and should be over as soon as possible. The freedom of movement, freedom to trade, freedom to enjoy ourselves in time off work, are all hard won and to be celebrated as achievements of a civilized society. But our commitment to maximizing the individual's accumulation of wealth is creating a noisy society which betrays the fact that we don't seem to have found fulfilment or peace in these freedoms. We have, instead, built economic systems of obligation that keep us on the roads even at four o'clock in the morning. The great cities of the world boast that they, like New York City in the song of the same name, 'never sleep': the lights are on and activity levels are still high during the night hours. I have sometimes spent nights taking part in multi-agency audits of people sleeping rough in London, and to walk around the streets in the early hours is a sobering experience. There is hardly any darkness, many people are working, making repairs to roads, cleaning buildings, maintaining essential services. Cab drivers are driving, buses are running, and, as we have discussed, the birds still sing.

Some economists, reflecting on what makes a thriving society, highlight environmental factors in their indices of wealth and poverty. One leading exponent of this is the Nobel Prize-winning economist Amartyr Sen. His work on human happiness, based on classic economic variables such as personal income, is being used in advising governments to take environmental factors into account when planning policy. The sound environment we create, much of which is traceable to our individual accumulation of wealth, invites reflection – not only spiritual, but academic – on what constitutes human flourishing.

A children's story tells of a Native American walking down a street in New York City. He turns to his companion and says, 'What a beautiful sound that cricket is making.' 'I can't hear it above all the traffic,' says his guide, 'how can you hear that?' 'It all depends what you're listening for,' says the Native American. As he says this, he takes a coin from his pocket and drops it on the pavement. A hundred heads turn towards the sound – of loose money.

The desert fathers and mothers identified a spiritual malaise described in Psalm 91. It is the 'pestilence that stalks by noonday'. *Accidie*, or *akedia*, is a spiritual listlessness, akin to boredom or exhaustion, and it strikes not during the dark night of the soul but in the daylight. It strikes when the sun is high and the light is strong – when we are busy and active and working hard. For businessmen and women, for overworked social workers, probation officers, teachers, call-centre workers, scientists, street cleaners, shift workers in our transport system, we have created a cityscape of perpetual noonday, of 24-hour helplines and all-night burger bars, and we wonder why our spirits are low. In the ancient world, a rhythm of fasting and feasting was connected to the rhythm of the earth or to large-scale events and disasters. In a never-ending feast without the fast, living in the day without a night, in light without darkness and noise without silence, our lament too takes a different form. It is hidden, unacknowledged, involuntary, but audible for those who listen to the signs of our times.

As we began with Rachel and Jephthah's daughter, we saw that, in the biblical tradition, an individual laments a personal loss, and one who laments can do so in response to a harsh situation on behalf of a whole people. If people are suffering, then their incentive to cry for change is great. As part of that cry for change, in Hebrew and Christian tradition, a lament is accompanied by fasting and weeping. But it may be that, in modern urban life, our collective lament takes a different form; this is a lament that accompanies not the fast but the feast. It is the sound of bewilderment as to what is 'enough'. How do we know when we've done enough, spent enough, bought enough? How do we cope with the seemingly relentless and unstoppable demands on our time and energy?

The ancient language of lament is in danger of becoming a lost language in a society that has made itself too busy to stop and face the forces of death that threaten to destroy it. The churches, in common with other world religions, do have the language of lament in their history and vocabulary but are afraid to speak it in case no one understands what is said.

The story was reported in 2007 of two Mexican brothers, the last remaining speakers of their local version of the language Zoque. They have stopped talking to each other for personal reasons, and so the language is in danger of dying out. I do wonder whether sometimes Christians aren't like that – arguing within the family and risking the extinction that can come with estrangement. The death of a language is not the death of speech itself – more will be said – but in a different tongue. It is the end of a people's journey – a fork in the road where one generation will always remain while the young travel further, taking the other path. For Christians and other peoples of faith, lament is one accent with which we speak our mother tongue, and in trying to listen for it and articulate it in a modern world, we need not be anxious. Fluency is neither a theological category nor a biblical imperative. Moses stammered; Paul was clearly not at all an impressive speaker; and when Peter spoke, although the crowd was 'cut to the heart', it was more likely to have been the passion and authenticity of this fisherman's voice that stirred them rather than the urbane rhetoric of his speech. Jesus was straightforward, even simplistic in his teaching about Christian communication with the world and with God. Do not worry about what you are to say when challenged by people, and do not heap up empty phrases when you're communicating with God.

The authentic lament of the Church, that is grounded in human experience now, will be heard by God and perhaps by a distracted world, which, in its own turn, reveals its grief in the lament of the sleepless city weeping for itself.

Notes

1. Walter Brueggemann, *A Commentary on Jeremiah: Exile and Homecoming*, Wm B. Eerdmans, 1998 p. 286.
2. Brueggemann, *A Commentary on Jeremiah*, pp. 287–8.
3. Mark Cazalet, *Seven Episodes from the Life of Mary for Our Lady of Lourdes*, Wanstead, www.markcazalet.co.uk.
4. Phyllis Trible, *Texts of Terror*, Augsberg Fortress, 1984.
5. Trible, *Texts of Terror*, chapter 4.
6. Billie Holiday, with William Duffy, *Lady Sings the Blues*, 1956; reprint Penguin, 1984, p. 84.
7. John White, *Billie Holiday: Her Life and Times*, Universe, 1987, p. 55.
8. Michael D. Coogan (ed.), *The Oxford Dictionary of the Biblical World*, Oxford University Press, 1998, p. 353.
9. For a closer discussion on lament in traditional societies, see Dr Andrea Fishman's research group at www.ihc.ucsb.edu/research/lament.html.
10. *New Scientist*, 4 December 2006.
11. *New Scientist*, 25 April 2007.
12. *New Scientist*, 22 August 2007.

CHAPTER 3

The Sound of Freedom

The liberation theologian Gustavo Gutiérrez reflected that, rather than focusing on what Jesus said on the cross, Christians should start by reflecting on the fact that he spoke at all. The fact that Christ cried out at the moment of his suffering is in itself teaching us about the nature of God in the midst of oppression and distress. As he was pinned to the cross, Jesus did not remain silent. In the face of torture and injustice, Jesus was not silent. Traditionally, Christians have described Jesus in terms of Isaiah's Suffering Servant, although biblical scholarship is divided on the matter of whether this refers to the Messiah or not. This picture, evocatively painted by Isaiah, is of one who, like a lamb before the shearers, does not open his mouth (Isaiah 53.7). The picture of Jesus silent in front of his accusers is a powerful one, his chosen vulnerability acting as an example in itself in his confrontation with human cruelty (cf. Matthew 26.63; Luke 23.9). Jesus' journey through the days before he died is the ultimate example of God's choosing to be silenced by the violent cruelty of humanity. But, after his silence before the court and the crowd, Jesus speaks. In liturgies and oratorios, we have tamed these cries and, perhaps because realism would never portray the depth of these utterances, the 'Seven Last Words' are usually intoned in rather more polite style than the originals. When we contemplate

Jesus on the cross outside a formal liturgical setting, we can imagine that he must have whispered, shouted, cried – and maybe he really, really cried, like a child alone, abandoned by God and out of reach of his mother who was below him, unable to touch or sooth his pain. However it happened, he voiced his feelings of despair and abandonment, and in doing so, taught us about God. To cry out when it seems that all is lost, to make a sound at all, reminds the one who suffers that they are still alive, that this will not last for ever, and in sounding this note, gives voice to the promise of freedom. The use of our voices in times of suffering is a strange kind of comfort. In the deepest sadness, you can hear someone crying, seemingly far away, and only realize after a while with a start that it is you.

Sound itself is not morally neutral, and, before we explore its power to liberate, it is right to acknowledge that it can also form part of the oppression. As we saw in the Introduction, it is not only with our ears that we listen. We use our whole bodies to experience sound and these nuances may be lost on those who are part of the hearing culture. On the other hand, distress may be caused to people with hearing impairments when an institution reinforces the collective experience of the hearing majority, without reference to those who are not part of hearing culture. In this case, liberation comes not so much by sound as from sound itself. This is a different way of describing our sound as our wound: it illustrates the fact that the Church, like other human institutions, is often capable of exclusion and betrayal. The Christian community is impoverished when it ignores a vital part of its own body. For example, preached sermons and discussion groups which interpret the story of Jesus' healing of the man in Mark 7 as a sign that a physical hearing impairment or loss is simply and universally something to be 'cured', reveal a wound of ignorance. The perspective of a Deaf Liberation theologian brings fresh wisdom to this Gospel for hearing people. The fact that Jesus touched the man on his ears and tongue communicated to him strong care and interest, in clear opposition to society's attitude, which was to ignore and exclude:

> ... and recognizes that it is not the deafness, the inability to hear, that needs to be healed but the inner damage caused by oppression. In referring to the man as going out and 'hearing' and 'speaking' it perhaps also relates an alternative vision of the future of deaf people, as visible and active in proclaiming the good news of Jesus Christ to all people, hearing and deaf.[1]

Inasmuch as enforced silence can suppress and exclude, so can sound for hearing people. Loud sound can cause hearing loss, and sound itself expresses values and maintains ideologies. Arguably, in a democracy there is no expressly articulated overarching political aim in controlling our sound environment (apart from reducing its volume), unlike in totalitarian regimes such as Nazi Germany, where Wagner and other Germanic composers were deemed 'great' and therefore a reinforcing cultural prop. It is easy to identify the explicit use of sound to achieve political ends (Tony Blair's New Labour campaign in 1997 became associated with its use of 'Things can only get better' by D:Ream) but to comment on the sound culture of a democracy where the aural environment seems more random, is difficult. One of the more dominant strands of sound in modern urban Britain, apart from transport, is advertising. In a mature market economy, buying and selling are key and prominent activities, and despite the efforts of successive governments, this spending creates a society that is ever more unequal. Studies are now beginning to show that in an unequal society, key indices of distress are noticeably higher. In *The Spirit Level: Why More Equal Societies Almost Always Do Better*,[2] Richard Wilkinson and Kate Pickett emphasize that it is not only those in poverty who suffer more from inequality. The whole of society is the poorer, rates of mental illness are higher, literacy rates are lower, and life expectancy is shorter. The three countries with the highest gap between rich and poor, and the greatest social and health problems are the UK, the USA and Portugal.

While eradicating absolute poverty has to be a serious priority for a civilized society, relative poverty, even when the basic needs of food and shelter are met, causes significant distress. To listen to a man in a bright jumper extolling, on television, the virtues of a hedge trimmer when you live on the sixteenth floor of a block of flats is a daily, even hourly, reminder that there is a world outside your door where people have hedges to trim. There is a loud party going on somewhere to which you are not invited. In a house where no one is working, constant advertising on the television or radio is a relentless reminder of exclusion. Sound has political meaning, and, in an unequal society, reinforces that inequality. Just like the Doppler effect of an ambulance whose sirens become discordant the further away it travels, the sound of affluence is very different when heard through the wall from far away. The buzz of conversation in a bar is intoxicating to the ones in the room, but to the young man walking past the window to the station, his redundancy letter in his pocket from the job he has only just started, it sounds like hell.

The collective experience of sound can be an oppressive or a liberating force, and there is one extreme way in which musical sound has been used to oppress and silence, and that is in the use of sound as torture. On the sixtieth anniversary of the Declaration of Human Rights, a new campaign was launched by musicians to protest against the practice of playing music as part of a regime of torture. The campaign, Zero dB, highlighted the practice of playing repetitive music loudly to 'soften' prisoners, to cause them significant distress and to create an aural environment from which there was absolutely no escape. Musicians whose music was used as a component in torture held one-minute silences at their concerts. The British singer David Gray commented:

> . . . what we're talking about is people in a darkened room, physically inhibited by handcuffs, bags over their heads and music blaring at them. That is nothing but torture. It doesn't matter what the music is. It could be Tchaikovsky's finest or it could be Barney the dinosaur. It doesn't really matter, it's going to drive you completely nuts.[3]

One former prisoner at Guantanamo Bay said that he had to listen to constant rock music. One band that featured heavily was the North American band Nine Inch Nails. Theirs is a mechanized sound with distorting guitars, metallic vocals and heavy repetitive bass, much loved by their devoted fanbase. If songs can be in themselves 'industrial', then they express something musically of the urban soundscapes discussed in Chapter 2. It is confident music, energetic in its monotones, with little variation in the melody (although there is melody), and almost inaudible lyrics. The effect of listening to this type of rock is like standing on the side of a musical motorway, with snippets of intelligible sound, or punctuating bass rhythm, but the overall impression is of an overwhelming wall of noise.

This same prisoner now says that he keeps his home 'very quiet' after saying too that the British band Queen's repetitive hit 'We Will Rock You' was also one of his musical tormenters.

But as David Gray commented, it wouldn't matter what kind of music was played, and the hard rock played was in contrast to other types of music, such as the simple melodic and repetitive themes from the children's programme *Sesame Street*. It is not that discordant music is in itself torturous. The use of melodic sound like David Gray, or Bruce Springsteen or *Sesame Street*, is fascinating in this context. As we have seen in Chapter 1 and will discuss in Chapter 5, for the early church writers, borrowing the theories of Boethius and Pythagorus, musical harmony was an indication of the presence of the angels and the heavenly powers, and it's dissonant sound that indicates something is wrong. In this case, that situation is reversed: harmonious, simple, melodic music like that played to help a child learn to read, becomes torturous in its repetition, volume and relentlessness. Silence, as we shall see later, for Hildegard of Bingen and the ancient Jewish apocalypse writers, indicated the presence of Satan. For these prisoners, it would have been a blessed relief. All is turned on its head in this use of music, and this perversion of harmony is more evidence, if any is needed, that the principle and practice of torture is not only wrong but blasphemous.

Robert Beckford has written of theorizing the politics of sound by reflecting on the sound-worlds of the dance hall and church hall. His concern is to 'construct a way of understanding sound in relation to the quest for gaining and maintaining power'.[4] He describes an experience when he was ten or eleven of being taken to a crowded converted classroom in the mid-1970s where the DJ was using the method of dub – an improvization method of mixing tracks. He reflects on this as an

... explicit politicization of sound – that is the audible artic- ulation of culture as a weapon in the struggle for justice and freedom in England by occupying the dance floor.[5]

Although this experience was new to him as a young man, the fact was that he felt comfortable with it. He explains this:

... intoxicated by sonic dominance and the physicality of the sound clash, I felt at home with the music, sound and culture of the event ... because I had been sensitized to these oral and physical aspects of Black life through worship at church.[6]

The point is that part of claiming his place in the struggle for justice and freedom was 'occupying the dance floor' and he felt confident to do that, because of his experience in church. It's a question we might usefully ask of all Christian communities – what is it in the sound-world of church that encourages con- fidence in us to join the struggle for liberation of all people in society?

The scriptural story of the Exodus – the Israelite journey from slavery to freedom – is the narrative that has inspired generations of Jews and Christians as they struggle to make sense of life in the world. The plagues visited on Egyptians and Israelites alike, followed by the drama of the night-time escape, with no time for bread to rise, the frantic fleeing from the pursuing Egyptians, the moment when it seemed all was lost as the Red Sea loomed in front of them, and the miracle of their crossing on dry land through the parted waves, have been the stuff of late-night stories, epic Hollywood films and a thou- sand whispered encouragements when spirits are low. At this pivotal point in the history of the people of Israel, the song of liberation is in the voice of the prophet Miriam (Exodus 15.21). It is she who leads the people in the song of deliverance from slavery and oppression. In listening for the scriptural sound of freedom, we listen to her. We first meet her as she stands at a distance, watching what will happen to her baby brother Moses who has been placed in the rushes by their mother (Exodus 2.4). She negotiates boldly with Pharaoh's daughter, finding a nurse for the boy, ensuring his survival and well-being. We next find her by the Red Sea leading the people in song and dance. But as the people spend time in the wilderness, we hear that Miriam and Aaron challenge Moses' authority (Numbers 12), and Miriam herself becomes ill and is put out of the camp. It seems that she has the people's support as they will not move on until she is brought back in, but we don't hear her prophetic voice again in the text, and she is buried in the wilderness of Zin, also known as Kadesh (Numbers 20.1). The biblical Miriam is a figure who knows personal suffering as well as the suffering of her people. We hear her strong voice in defence of a defenceless child, in leadership and celebration of freedom, and in challenge to human authority. She is silenced by disease, dishonour and death, and for a woman whose story irrigates the prophecy of her brother Moses by her interventions at the River Nile and the Red Sea, it is an irony that she dies in a dry land where there was no water.[7]

In the tradition of Miriam, expressing a previously hidden experience of exclusion and slavery has, for movements of liberation, been described as finding a voice. Sometimes that will be a physical voice, or a metaphorical voice, but the analogy is an evocative one. It is one of the few powers left to a prisoner. To cry out, to speak, to shout, to sing. The diaries of eighteenth-century white slave owners in the southern states of America reveal complaints that they were kept up all night by slaves singing, no doubt songs that told the story of the Exodus of old.

Excluded peoples have found a voice, sometimes in music, sometimes in speech, and, as we have seen, sometimes in signs and fresh interpretations of Scripture. The metaphor of finding your voice has been particularly strong for women and for people of colour. And this plays out in the Church as well as in society as a whole.

In an idle moment during a church service, it's worth looking to see who has written the music and the words for the liturgy. The word 'liturgy' means 'the work of the people' – and so I am often intrigued to see who these people are. There are many names that come up time after time – in the hymns we sing, the Wesley brothers of course feature – with words and tunes. If it's a service with a choir, they may sing something by Mozart or Thomas Tallis, or in a cathedral a splendid Mass setting by anyone from William Byrd to the contemporary composers John Rutter or James McMillan. If it's a service with worship songs, we may sing something by Graham Kendrick or Matt Redman; if it is an evening meditative service, we may sing some Iona songs by John Bell or a chant or two by Brother Roger and the community at Taizé.

Although women cantors and organists or pianists often play in church communities Sunday by Sunday, the truth is that not many women write music that shapes the musical language of the Church. It is overwhelmingly male, still, in an age when it really doesn't have to be.[8] In the development of early Christian theology, music and singing itself became associated with the feminine, and thus became something of which to be very suspicious. Strongly influenced by Greek ideas of harmony and order in the universe, Augustine, Aquinas and

John Chrysostom all viewed music with caution. The sounds of the music itself – and I'm not just talking about the text that is sung – were the problem. At a time when there was deep disagreement about whether music should be used at all in worship, Augustine was anxious:

> When it happens to me that the music moves me more than the subject of the song, I confess myself to commit a sin deserving punishment, and then I would prefer not to hear the singer.[9]

But then again,

> I remember being told often of Bishop Athanasius of Alexandria. He used to make the Reader of the psalm chant with so flexible a speech-rhythm that he was nearer to reciting than to singing. Nevertheless, when I remember the tears which I poured out at the time when I was first recovering my faith, and that now I am moved not by the chant but by the words being sung, when they are sung with a clear voice and entirely appropriate modulation, then again I recognize the great utility of music in worship.[10]

Augustine struggles with his reaction to music – he feels he has to confess his emotional reaction, and his ambivalence towards the music itself and determination to focus on the text persist today. Musical enjoyment is associated with bodily enjoyment, and therefore set against spiritual fulfilment. At a time when femininity was closely associated with the material, and masculinity with the spiritual, and thus privileged, St Paul's injunction that women should not speak in church meant that women should not only not preach, but should not sing either. All hints of femininity in music-making were to be avoided. In the twelfth century, a Cistercian statute of 1134 described the ideal music of the Church:

> . . . it befits men to sing with a manly voice, and not in a womanish manner with tinkling, . . . with 'false' voices, as if imitating the wantonness of minstrels.[11]

This was released at the same time as the astonishing abbess and composer Hildegard of Bingen was doing precisely the opposite. She was innovative not only in that she wrote chants for her sisters to sing themselves, but in the musical intervals she used. Her freedom to write new chants was unparalled in the Middle Ages. She used a wide range (sometimes up to two octaves), large leaps and elaborate melodies. She often opened her melodies with an ascending open fifth (the same interval that begins the Last Post on Remembrance Sunday) and her texts were of concern for the earth and in praise of God as Creator. Her music was a song of freedom in a church which banned her chants in 1178 and her sisters from singing them. Despite this silencing, she was arguably the first Christian leader, male or female, to forge a link between her music and her theology.[12]

Hildegard based her compositions on hours of singing, intuitive experimentation with intervals, and themes from her mystical visions. She wrote music from her direct experience of the love of God, and in doing so, wrote songs of freedom in a closed world. In Hildegard's eighteen-part piece *Ordo Virtutum*, the character of Mary sings a full octave plus a sixth (a huge range), and when Adam and Eve are expelled from the Garden of Eden, it is not Eve who is blamed, as was traditional, but Satan. Moreover, it is Satan who is incapable of song and who is responsible for the silencing of Adam. Her conception of Satan was that of the silencer. She also had a strong sense, similar to the reflections offered by Evelyn Glennie, that the whole human body is a musical instrument. It is not simply our vocal cords that enable us to sing, just as it is not only with our ears that we listen. She described herself as God's trumpet:

> I at times, resound a little, like a small trumpet note from the living brightness.[13]

Hildegard was ahead of her time in developing an incarnational theology in music: she argued that the whole human body was a musical instrument, and this is not just for the musically talented. The resonances, rhythms and melodies of our bodies are the pipes and strings on which is played out the story of our lives. It has often struck me that babies scream and cry much more than the average adult, but they never lose their voice. The process of growing up is often accompanied by our acquiring more tension, placing constraints on our voices because of the restriction of our shoulder, neck and jaw. As adults, we often tell stories of when we were thrown out of the school choir, or told that we just couldn't sing. There is a clear association between natural aptitude for music and the 'rightness' of making it. Many of us adults say, in the way that we say about maths, that we can't sing, we were never any good at it. It becomes part of our identity – we become people who don't sing (except maybe in the shower or the car) and it doesn't occur to us that this can change. But it can, and our whole bodies become musical instruments when we are released from the tension we acquire as adults and learn to sing.

Two groups of young people are sounding significant notes of liberation as the twenty-first century begins. They are coming from two areas of the world more readily associated with severe poverty or intractable conflict.

The sounds of liberation, and even of musical revolution, are audible in the inspirational playing of the Simon Bolivar National Youth Orchestra from Venezuela. In a performance of Bernstein's *Symphonic Dances* at the Proms in 2007, the players – all aged between 18 and 25 – did not sit demurely as other classical orchestral players do, observing the conventions of modern concert etiquette. They moved with the music, waved their violins in the air and spun their double basses during their 'rests'. They 'danced' in their seats as they played, and the energy with which they perform music from Mahler to 'Mambo' is infectious, communicating an intense emotional maturity beyond their years. This is no ordinary orchestra, as the musicians in it have come through a radical music education project 'El Sistema', founded by the extraordinary musician (and economist) José Antonio Abreu. His scheme gives young people living in poverty in Venezuela access to classical music teaching. His philosophy is that music cannot be hidden from the people within a cultural elite and that music is a social right. He told *The Guardian* newspaper in 2006,

> The philosophy of El Sistema shows that the vicious circle of poverty can be broken when a child poor in material possessions acquires spiritual wealth through music.

He began with just eleven boys, although he had been donated 50 music stands. He commented that the choice before him was either to give back the stands or attract more children.

Today there are about a quarter of a million children involved in 'El Sistema' studying their instruments not so much alone as in ensembles and orchestras, learning the emotional and technical interdependence on which ensemble playing relies. Their performances are exuberant, serious minded, technically excellent and, somehow, kind. The head of music at the South Bank Centre at the time of their residence in spring 2009 predicted:

> Anyone who ever thought classical music was not for them – this is the one thing they should see. They demonstrate what we've perhaps been missing in Europe – musicians performing out of a sheer goddamn unbridled desire to live the music.[14]

As their conductor, Gustavo Dudamel, himself a product of the system, likes to say, they play as if they are playing each piece for the first – or the last – time.

The very fact that children born into poverty are becoming world-renowned classical musicians immediately challenges the assumption that excellence relies on elitism. Classical music has developed a cultural meaning which makes it 'high art' and therefore out of reach to children of the slums. But there is nothing intrinsically elitist about it, and all that is required to enjoy it is a passion for melody, the teaching and encouragement of others, and persistence to learn the skill. The principles of 'El Sistema' are inspiring similar music projects in London, Manchester and Liverpool. By breaking the conventions of how classical music 'should' be taught and played, the Venezuelan orchestra continues to make sounds of liberation, allowing their exuberant commitment to beauty to set themselves and others free.

The West–Eastern Divan Orchestra is, in a different way, sounding notes of liberation and reconciliation in the Middle East. The conductor Daniel Barenboim began the experimental group of Israeli and Palestinian musicians in 1999. Now the orchestra travels all over the world and is much sought after in leading concert venues. Barenboim himself commented:

> Music, unlike any other art or discipline, requires the ability to express oneself with absolute commitment and passion while listening carefully and sensitively to another voice which may even contradict one's own statement. The same two young people who might encounter each other at a checkpoint in the roles of border guard and citizen under occupation sit next to one another in this orchestra, playing the same music, equally striving for perfection of musical expression, and equally responsible for the result.[15]

The very act of making music together is a protest against the inequalities and divisions that human beings create and re-create in every century. It is not diversionary activity from the 'real' world of politics or economics, but is in itself a political act when such beauty is created by young people like these and many others in music therapy projects and housing estate choirs and instrumental groups all over the world.

In recording the story of the movement from silence to sound, from restriction to liberation, there is no better collection of sounds through which to do this than jazz.

The relationship between Christian faith and jazz music has not been straightforward, since jazz grew out of its nineteenth-century gospel roots to become a new way of making music in the early twentieth century in America. Although the music sounds melodic, it was highly controversial in its own day –

not so much for the genre but for the fact that the same person would sing about faith in God and their experience of the world. For conservative churchgoers, Sister Wynona Carr (1924–76) and other artists such as Sister Rosetta Tharpe and Marie King were crossing an unacceptable line by singing gospel music and also jazz or blues. Wynona Carr (the 'Sister' was reportedly added by her producer to make her more appealing to the gospel audience) recorded some revolutionary versions of classics in the 1940s, although the studios didn't release them as they were considered to be too controversial. She recorded a heavily jazz-influenced version of a gospel hit, 'Our Father', although the one that was released to the public was much more conservative.[16] She didn't receive the recognition she deserved in her lifetime, although later stars such as Aretha Franklin acknowledged their debt to her. She was truly a musical pioneer, a composer who felt free, not unlike Hildegard, to write lyrics and improvise music that was ahead of her day both in the Church and in the music world. The swinging of her song 'In a Little While' has a driving rhythm that makes you want to get up out of your seat and move to it. It's not music to listen to or sing alone – its energy gives it the feeling of a revival meeting. It's not long until the trials of life will be over, and we will be free: and it's not just an individual dream, it's hope for all God's people.

From these gospel singers crossing over into the secular music world, jazz became the primary genre of music through which to express the complexities of personal love and relationships. In the songs of B. B. King, Ella Fitzgerald, Louis Armstrong and Frank Sinatra, expression was given to sometimes very subtle moments in personal relationships, and the thoroughly human feelings of jealousy, rejection and betrayal were brought into the light. The genre of jazz can give voice to these difficult and complex emotions with its melancholy tunes, its sense that even when the singer is singing about love, they express something of the essential aloneness of our lives. And the way in which jazz expresses that heartache is because it is *lived* music.

We learn in this music of our vulnerability, our woundedness, when we expose ourselves to love and its power. Living in love is always a risk, and in its tradition of improvization, jazz music expresses this well. The chord structure underneath the melody remains the same, but improvizing takes a risk in creating something in the moment that is new and that may not work. There are decisive moments in our lives: when we move into a new situation that can't be reversed; when we have children; when we make vows or when we fall in love for the first time; when we lose someone we love – something changes in us for ever. But we still live day to day – improvizing life – making it up as we go along. The familiar chords – the building-blocks of our lives – underpin us, but we find our own tune and sing with our own voice.

Jazz expresses things that are deeply personal – it brings out the private fears, desires, complexities of human relationships – and sings them out for all of us to recognize. In that way, it is performing something of a religious function; it is taking the stuff of our lives – our search for someone to love for example, or our hopes for a better world – and giving them form and beauty, rhyme and rhythm, so that as we listen, we know somehow that we are not alone. In any love story true to itself, the themes of betrayal, yearning, rejection and loss are an inevitable part of it. Traditional Christian teaching has often found honest expression of these deeply personal feelings difficult, and explicitly Christian words and music tends to suppress these ideas in favour of broader themes such as love, joy, self-control. It is there in the Hebrew tradition, in the Song of Songs, in the love story between Jacob and Rachel. But in the New Testament there is less evidence that people are falling in love, having romantic and sexual relationships, getting hurt, finding someone new. Jazz music gives explicit expression to these complex themes and names our loneliness; and when we have named it, we are free. In Genesis, Jacob wrestled with the angel, and at the end of the night-long struggle he begged to know the angel's name. Jazz, like no other sound, names the heartache, the weak-kneed surprise, the delight, fury and jealousy that go hand in hand with the search for human love, and by giving it expression, relieves the loneliness of life in the world. Ironically, in singing about our loneliness, we reduce its power and give voice to the melodies of longing for connection and love.

The blues have an even more explicit history of liberation. A movement in musical form was heralded by early blues singers such as Bessie Smith and Robert Johnson. The spirituals sung by slaves as work songs were essentially collective experiences: choruses and chants with solid, regular rhythms to be sung together when working on repetitive tasks. Blues, emerging in the immediate post-slave decades, was music to be sung by one person, a free person, accompanied in the early days by one instrument: perhaps a guitar or a banjo. In this way, the freedom of an individual to sing alone was itself a political act: singing out the life experience of emancipated slaves for all to hear.

Blues singers developed particular characteristics in their singing. They not only improvised around a melody as in jazz, but they also started to 'bend' the notes. If you imagine a piano keyboard, and the white and black notes on it, blues singers slide between these notes. They sing microtones: Charles Ives called it 'singing in the cracks'. These microtones convey powerful emotion – more like a howl or a wail. It is strong, and carries the weight of protest against generations of slavery and poverty. It sounds like not only a cry for, but a resolute statement of, freedom. While early male blues singers like Robert Johnson were singing of their dead or struggling mothers, or of the temptation of drink or no-good women, women blues singers were also singing about their lives. They were free for the first time to sing about society, even in a society where they could not vote.

The most outstanding blues singer of her day was Bessie Smith (1895–1937). At six feet tall and weighing fifteen stone, Bessie Smith was a formidable figure on stage and in blues history. She came from a preacher's family and her mother died when she was a child. Strong and independent, Bessie Smith was singing before microphones were used regularly, and so she projected her voice naturally over the backing band without any problem. The musician Mae Barnes remembered,

> Bessie used to wear the most fabulous costumes. Birds of paradise all in her hair. Along the sides of her gowns there were feathers sticking out from everywhere. Then she changed and wore evening gowns with beads and rhinestones; they were popular in those days. No sequins, but just beads, beads, loads of beads and rhinestones, big rhinestones.[17]

Bessie Smith performed songs which articulated a strong critique of the economic and social status of black Americans in the immediate post-slavery decades. In her pioneering song 'Poor Man's Blues' of 1928 she focuses on the different status of women between white and black:

Mister rich-man, open your heart and mind;
Give the poor man a chance, help stop these hard,
    hard times.
While you're livin' in your mansion you don't know
    what hard times means.
Poor working man's wife is starvin', your wife is livin'
    like a queen.[18]

She sang strong imaginative lyrics, describing a fictitious yet familiar place where everything is upside down, not how it should be:

Back in Black Mountain, a child will smack your face
Babies cryin' for liquor, and all the birds sing bass.[19]

Bessie Smith wrote songs about domestic violence, poverty, isolation and death, and her tone was that of an independent, strong-willed protagonist, not a helpless victim. The strength of her sound, together with stories of her facing down the Ku Klux Klan,[20] give us a sense of her scorn for the society that refused her equality with white men or women. She and her co-writers named the double jeopardy that black women faced in the post-slavery decades, and not even the Klan could silence her voice.

In 1907 Alberta Hunter ran away to Chicago aged twelve as she had heard she could make ten dollars a week singing.

The blues? Why, the blues are a part of me. They're like a chant. The blues are like spirituals, almost sacred. When we sing blues, we're singing out our hearts, we're singing out our feelings. Maybe we're hurt and just can't answer back, then we sing or maybe even hum the blues. When I sing,

'I walk the floor, wring my hands and cry – Yes, I walk the floor, wring my hands and cry' . . . what I'm doing is letting my soul out.[21]

Alberta Hunter's comment that even she will sometimes hum the blues delineates the fact that making the smallest sound can be a protest and a solace in trouble. Letting your soul out brought freedom within a tightly constricted life.

The blues and jazz can be sung by anyone who is willing to understand the protest and lament it carries, and the debt owed by later white musicians such as Eric Clapton is acknowledged by them. But the roots of this music are firmly in the particular historical experience of freed slaves, and their voices carry down the years, challenging us to listen to this sound of struggle for dignity and freedom. In honouring this sound, we can join God's work of justice, healing and peace for men, women and children, regardless of skin colour, nationality or creed. More jazz should be part of church culture, not only because it tells the story of the Exodus in a powerful way, but because it addresses precisely those areas of life that church communities often find difficult to handle: romantic yearning, lust, jealousy, violence, political and social injustice. In the acknowledgement of the particular story which jazz and blues represent, and in the form of the music itself, with its emphasis on improvization, it is, for me, the best musical expression of human liberation in the world.

I want to end with one story which is personal. At the end of my time at university, I spent two weeks in the company of a close friend to witness a remarkable transformation. I was there to accompany him as he went through an intensive course of speech therapy for a condition he learned later was called puberphonia. For the whole of our time as friends at college, and despite his being 21, his voice was that of a pre-pubescent boy. He was lively, much loved and with lots of friends, but he dreaded meeting new people as he saw the shock flick across their face when he spoke for the first time. He had attended an all-boys school, and in classes, through his formative teenage years, had 'basically not answered any questions for five years'. He was intelligent, friendly and intensely musical, but was afraid to speak in academic or social situations because of the reaction of his peers. All of this was deeply traumatic, and so on the whole his fear kept him silent. He developed a phobia of the phone and avoided answering or making calls as he was always assumed by the person on the other end to be female. After several years of visits to different speech therapists, he discovered that treatment for this condition was not a physical operation, but a short course of intensive therapy, and so the decision to have treatment to change his voice was now an option. But it was not entirely straightforward. Whatever trauma he suffered from watching others react to a grown man speaking in a boy's voice, whatever distress he felt when he was constantly assumed to be a woman on the phone, it was also a part of his identity. He knew that another, more mature voice was in his body because he could cough or shout in a much lower register. But he couldn't speak all the time in this voice. His adult self hid underneath the high voice of a child. To choose to change must have been, as well as exciting, an alarming experience. I once asked him whether he had ever spoken to anyone else who had this condition. His answer startled me and highlighted the extent of his isolation. He had never met anyone with this condition, although he had been served once in a shop with someone he thought might have it. He didn't say anything at the time, as you wouldn't to a stranger, but the fact that there had been only one fleeting, anonymous encounter with someone who might know, really know what it was like, I found very moving.

I was there over those summer weeks to attend sessions with the speech therapist with him, to listen to what happened and to the exercises he was given, and then to be with him the rest of the time in the 'outside world', remembering with him all the points she had made. My role was as an extra memory, and perhaps a small pot of extra courage to help him put into practice what he was doing in the therapist's room. The first time he went into a shop I stood outside as he tried to make himself go in and buy a newspaper. We discussed what he would say to people he knew well before he phoned them so that they could hear his 'new voice'. It was an immense privilege to be allowed to accompany someone through such an emotional change, and I observed in him that to speak with a completely different voice seemed to be at once frightening and exhilarating. The truth was that the sound he was making was cavernous and strange to him – it felt unfamiliar and disorientating – but to the outside world it was totally unremarkable. One of the most amazing moments was in the speech therapist's room when he tried out his deep voice for the first time. She showed us on a screen the pitch level of the noise he was making – and asked him to choose where (that is, how deep) he wanted to have his new voice. He tried different levels, overcompensating at first and sounding a bit like Paul Robeson played at the wrong speed, but eventually settling for a resonant bass sound that he has until this day.

This in itself would be a wonderful story of liberation, but there's more. Now, he is a professional singer, a counter tenor (also known as a male alto), and a member of one of the top early-music ensembles in the world. His singing voice is the highest of the male voices and is in exactly the same register as his previous speaking voice. When he sings in this high register, he not only brings Renaissance polyphony alive, he delights audiences from Sydney Opera House to Japanese concert halls and the best London venues. It is precisely this speaking voice which kept him silent for so many years, which now is set gloriously free to sing polyphony – music that in its delicacy and unaccompanied harmony brings healing to a broken world. And just to complete the picture, his freelance career has been built on his constantly answering his mobile phone.

Sound is a potent element in the battle for human liberty. It is used to oppress and subdue, to exclude and to harm. It is also a powerful weapon in the struggle for freedom. In the tradition of Miriam and Moses leading their people to freedom and singing out the liberation they found, individuals and peoples on every continent and in every century find a voice in the depth of their suffering to protest against the pain. In doing so, they follow the example of Jesus, whose silence was broken as he was pinned to the cross. His expression of human need, of forgiveness of his torturers, of abandonment by God in the hours before his death, teaches us courage to claim the freedom that is ours. We learn that, when we find our own true voice and use it, we set ourselves and others free.

Notes

1. Hannah Lewis, *Deaf Liberation Theology*, Ashgate, 2007, p. 149.
2. Published by Allen Lane, 2009.
3. Duncan Campbell, *The Guardian*, Thursday, 11 December 2008.
4. Robert Beckford, *Jesus Dub*, Routledge, 2006, p. 15.
5. Beckford, *Jesus Dub*, pp. 16–17.
6. Beckford, *Jesus Dub*, p. 17.

7. Phyllis Trible, 'Bringing Miriam Out of the Shadows', *Bible Review*, February 1989, quoted in Miriam Therese Winter, *Woman Wisdom*, Collins Dove, 1991.

8. There are notable contemporary exceptions: for example, June Boyce Tilman and the tradition of Free Church women hymnwriters, but the minorities are still small.

9. Augustine, *Confessions* XXXiii (50), trans. Henry Chadwick, Oxford University Press, 1992.

10. Augustine, *Confessions* XXXiii (50), p. 208.

11. Quoted in Heidi Epstein, *Melting the Venusberg*, Continuum, 2004, p. 36.

12. Epstein, *Melting the Venusberg*, pp. 120–34.

13. Hildegard, in Dronke, 'Women Writers of the Middle Ages', in Epstein, *Melting the Venusburg*, pp. 197, 217ff.

14. Marshall Marcus, *The Guardian*, 27 February 2009.

15. Daniel Barenboim, *The Guardian*, 13 December 2008.

16. *Dragnet for Jesus*, recorded 1949–54, released on the Speciality label; re-released Ace Records, 1992.

17. Quoted in *Wild Women Don't Have the Blues* documentary by Calliope Film Resources website, 'The Classic Blues and the Women Who Sang Them'. Copyright 2000 CFR, http://www.calliope.org/blues/blues2.html, 29 April 2009.

18. 'Poor Man's Blues', Columbia 14399-D, 24 August 1928, reissued on *Empty Bed Blues*, Columbia CG 30450, 1972, quoted in Angela Y. Davis, *Blues Legacies and Black Feminism*, Vintage Books, 1998.

19. 'Black Mountain Blues', Columbia 14554-D, 22 June 1930, reissued on *The World's Greatest Blues Singer*, Columbia CG 33, 1972, quoted in Davis, *Blues Legacies and Black Feminism*, p. 264.

20. See Davis, *Blues Legacies and Black Feminism*, p. 37.

21. Quoted in *Wild Women Don't Have the Blues* documentary by Calliope Film Resources website, 'The Classic Blues and the Women Who Sang Them.' Copyright 2000 CFR, http://www.calliope.org/blues/blues2.html. 29 April 2009.

CHAPTER 4

The Sound of Resurrection

It was 7 p.m. on Good Friday at St Paul's Cathedral. The services for the day were over. Thousands of people had come throughout the day to wait by the foot of the huge, life-sized (or rather death-sized) wooden cross set up under the dome. We had listened again to the story of betrayal and fear, and been transported to first-century Palestine where we heard the cries of desolation from a tortured man and the Temple curtain ripping in two. We had felt grateful when, at the end of the exhausting Passion story, Joseph of Arimathea had arrived and in the murmured tones of the political elite, used to negotiation, arranged for Jesus to be laid in a borrowed tomb after the ravages of the day.

Back in the twenty-first century, the sun, setting over London, had streamed through the west window a couple of hours earlier, spotlighting the cross and making the congregation gasp with the drama of it all. Tomorrow night we would light a new fire, wear new clothes, and with singing and acclamation announce once again that the despair of this day was transfigured by a love the like of which the world had never known. Those of us who were there were physically and mentally tired, having travelled through Holy Week, not just listening to the old story but being confronted with the contemporary themes of cruelty and cowardice in a suffering world.

I watched two workmen approach the huge wooden cross set up under the dome in order to move it, ready for the next day. I knew that it would be placed by the font, and it would be transformed from an instrument of death into a symbol of life by beautiful and fragrant flowers. I almost turned away, exhausted by the hours spent gazing at the hard wood. But I wasn't prepared for what then happened. The two men, instead of carrying the cross, or detaching it from its base, realized that it was too large to pick up, even for both of them. Instead, they put their backs into it and started to push. As they gained momentum the cross simply flew the whole length of the long aisle, fleeing, it seemed, from the fixed, stuck, exposed place where Jesus died, and looking as if at any moment it would crash through the vast locked doors and escape into the city. It was as if a butterfly, pinned on a board for people to stare at, had suddenly smashed upwards through its glass case, and had flown high in the sky out of reach, sunlight catching the reinvigorated colour on its delicate wings. This moment of release, this sudden movement and freedom, made sense for me of the ancient words of John of Damascus that Christ 'burst his tomb', and that resurrection is the 'spring of souls'.

The centuries melted away and the anonymous medieval writer who imagined the cross itself as a witness to Christ's death, spoke again in my mind's ear.

> It seemed I saw the tree itself
> borne on the air, light wound about it,
> a beam of brightest wood, a beacon clad
> in overlapping gold, glancing gems
> fair at its foot, and fine stones
> set in a crux flashed from the crosstree.[1]

Resurrection is not an easy or obvious concept to describe, and biblical interpreters, along with artists, poets and musicians, have struggled to depict it well. When trying to depict the afterlife, paintings and mosaics of hell are often much more vivid than imagined pictures of heaven, which end up being rather limp pastoral scenes compared with the energy and colour of the damned. Resurrection is an inexplicable transformation, and the best we can say about it is that it is a life that is lived after death. The Christian understanding of resurrection conflates earlier Jewish ideas of Ezekiel's dry bones living, with later ideas of eternal spiritual life. Resurrection in Christ has become the gateway to that eternal life, although in its Jewish origins the resurrection of the body didn't carry that meaning.[2] St Paul's resonant phrases in his first letter to the Corinthians (15.51–57) describe what happened at the resurrection as a victory. Death is 'swallowed up' and God has 'given us the victory' by raising Jesus. Paul's language to the Corinthians is that of domination, and casts Jesus as a conquering hero. After the submission of God in Christ to the violence of human beings in crucifixion, the meaning of resurrection is that God's dominance over death is re-established.

A highly successful art exhibition was held at the National Gallery in 2000 entitled 'Seeing Salvation'. I wondered at the time what it would be like to *hear* it. From Handel's *Messiah*, we hear one imaginative interpretation of the sound of resurrection that comes straight from Paul's letter to the Corinthians itself: that 'the trumpet shall sound and the dead shall be raised'. The trumpet imagery is found in other New Testament texts too. In 1 Thessalonians 4, resurrection happens 'at the call of the archangel and the trumpet of God', and in these texts resurrection is linked with judgement. In a natural sound environment, as early as 1500 BCE when trumpets were undoubtedly used in China and Egypt, the notes of a trumpet must have been one of the loudest manufactured sounds available to a writer imagining the end of the world. In military situations, the sound of a trumpet is decisive: it changes the action of those who hear it. It signals a decision, a moment of crisis, a command to move. In Handel's music, the trumpet in the orchestra embellishes the bass aria with staccato dotted notes, reminiscent of a military call to arms. It is a sound designed to stiffen the Christian sinews, make us stand up straight and claim the triumph won by our leader.

I have always had trouble with much of the conventional Christian imagery around resurrection. I struggle with the military triumphalism in victory, which doesn't seem to me to ring true. I have never met any member of the armed forces who displayed triumphalism in victory. It is much more likely that men and women who have been at war describe the fight as hellish, and in victory it is the memory of those who were lost that fills their minds. I have sometimes struggled too with Paul's territorial language of Romans 5 and 6. The fact that death has no 'dominion' has rarely touched my heart, although intellectually I can follow the analogy. The language is still that of a sovereign ruler victorious in battle, and this pre-modern world-view doesn't make me want to join Christ's army. But however much I struggle with it, I don't want to discard these powerful images, as I learned when preparing teenagers in a rough area of town for baptism and confirmation. As we talked about the battle imagery and the strongly worded promise to renounce evil, I was expecting them to dismiss the medieval pictures that the Church presented to them as so much mumbo-jumbo. On the contrary, they immediately translated the language into meaningful discussion about the dangers of drugs at the school gate and began to talk about what it was like trying to stand up to bullying or trying to get good marks when no one thought they could. The battle was joined every day for them, and my assumptions about relevance and resonance in their lives were wrong. However, in acknowledging the victory and dominion language used about Jesus in resurrection, it is not the only way to interpret what happened when he died and therefore what happens to us.

There are many artistic expressions of crucifixion, and there are many musical representations of the agony of Christ. But there are fewer depictions visually or aurally of resurrection. It's as if the human imagination is more acutely tuned to suffering than glory. Scripture gives us vivid pictures of the trial and crucifixion of Christ, and tells us of the miraculous encounters men and women had with Jesus after the resurrection, but it too is remarkably silent on the matter of resurrection itself. The only Gospel to attempt to describe the resurrection is Matthew's. There is an earthquake, and an angel descends from heaven and rolls the stone away, seemingly in the presence of Mary Magdalene and the other Mary. The angel sits on the stone and the guards are so afraid they shake and become like dead men (Matthew 28.4). The body of Jesus, however, has already gone.

In the other Synoptic Gospels and in John, this crucial moment in the relationship between God and humanity happens 'off stage', away from the narrative where we don't see it. What we do notice are the consequences of resurrection, and the dramatic change in the behaviour of those who were there.

In the liturgical language of the Church, it is a challenge to bring this part of the Passion story to life – defined as it is by the absence rather than the presence of Jesus. We listen to the message of the angels saying 'He is not here' and wonder how to tell a sceptical society about an empty tomb. After the hustle and bustle of the betrayal and trial, what can we say about resurrection?

When Western Christians go on pilgrimage to the Holy Land, groups walk the way of the Cross through the streets of Jerusalem, and often it is the noise of modern-day Jerusalem that pilgrims find distracting, or distasteful. Guides explain to the groups that, far from being distracted by the postcard sellers and shouting of street traders, in this chaotic jostling they are experiencing as authentic an experience of first-century Palestine as they can get. One of the most striking things about Mel Gibson's film *The Passion of the Christ*, apart from the gratuitous violence, was its hustle and noise, not to mention the variety of languages, highlighting the political reality of occupation and the context of Jesus' execution. The sounds of the film were as revelatory as the sights, and reminded us, in a startling way, of the cultural filters through which we view the life of Christ.

As part of the Christian observance of Holy Week, many churches bring the Passion narratives alive with sound in a way we rarely do at other times of the year. We don't have difficulty imagining the hammer-blows of the soldiers as nails are driven into flesh, and we re-create this sound for Passion plays and services. We often stage dramatic readings of the story, with congregations in church or outside on the street playing the part of the crowd, reminding us of the fickle nature of crowds and our complicity in public acclamation and condemnation. Resurrection itself seems to be silent: a delicate, unheard moment of grace that, when we finally notice it, we realize has been there all the time. The first sound of resurrection we hear is a woman's name: 'Mary'. This tender conversation between Jesus and Mary Magdalene is the dominant visual image of resurrection repeated by artists over centuries. After a faltering conversation full of mistakes and misunderstandings, she is told to go and teach her brothers the greatest truth about God. We imagine the consternation among the disciples, the argument and scepticism, and eventually the hurried footsteps of two of them running across town to find the tomb and see for themselves.

One classic depiction of this moment is Titian's *Noli me Tangere* which was a highlighted feature of the 'Seeing Salvation' exhibition mentioned earlier. Much was written at the time about the success of the National Gallery's exhibition, in a city in which large numbers of people no longer recognize the Christian narrative. Christian commentators identified a lingering interest – or perhaps even more than that, a thirst – to experience the greatest story ever told, and it is a story which, rooted in art, engages all our senses. As well as the colour and texture of figurative painting, a good painter will communicate not just picture but sound.

The picture on the front cover of this book is 'The Scream' by Edvard Munch. It is, for me, both a noisy and a quiet painting, because the scream is silent. While the sound-waves seem to permeate the very contours of the environment, distorting all that surrounds it, the scream is apparently not heard by the people walking over the bridge in the background. In my mind, the androgenous character whose ears are covered and whose mouth is forming the wound through which the scream might come, is mysteriously unable to give voice to the mixture of pain, ecstasy and intensity that might constitute sound. In this way, the creature *is* the sound, the scream, not just the host for it or the author of it. I spent hours in front of this painting in Oslo National Art Gallery one cold afternoon in November. I was myself in mental pain over something that had recently happened, and in contemplating this painting, and trying to hear it, the scream became at once a cry of solidarity with me in my misery, and also, by its very expression, comfort to my aching soul. The fact that my own heart was breaking found expression and a home in the figure in the foreground, crouched over while everyone else walked on by. It wasn't at all depressing – I was not driven into deeper despair, quite the opposite. Somehow I was understood, the burden became bearable and I was able to walk back onto the street.

As an object in physical reality, a painting is itself a flat, silent object. It takes a special artist to depict, in this medium, a sound like screaming. Trying to paint a sound is itself a paradoxical experience that fuses our sensory experience and our imaginative engagement with the art. It's like writing down the word 'blue' using red ink. It is like shouting the word 'silence'. It's like reaching out to touch the air. It is itself a paradox and makes straightforward description impossible.

Perhaps the most well-known artistic portrayals of resurrection have been painted by the early-twentieth-century artist Stanley Spencer. 'The Resurrection, Cookham', painted between 1924 and 1926, was greeted with great praise when it was shown for the first time. The scene is the churchyard at Cookham in Berkshire. Graves are opening, and people from different generations and centuries are emerging. A girl smells a flower, a woman brushes down her husband's jacket. There are no heralds or trumpets here, and when one looks at this painting, it may be that you imagine the conversation between the people who emerge, some of them after centuries of silence. Reaching across hundreds of years, the boy from 1920 might say all sorts of things to an Elizabethan noblewoman.

But examining the painting closely, each person has closed lips. No one is speaking. The scene sounds a blissful stillness, a rapturous, timeless quietness.

Resurrection for Spencer was something that could happen

> . . . anywhere on the street: out of the gutters a lady magnificently attired would push the lid off a manhole & step out, some would come up from under the drawing room carpet or the floor boards of the kitchen, others would stroll out the side of a hill or emerge from a heap of wheat in a barn. . . . Some would come through the centre of a billiard table or a committee room table & and the members of the committee would kneel & pray & assist. Children would sometimes resurrect among mushroom rings & among rubbish heaps & among clumps of Kingcups & among the shingle of shallow slow running streams or out of the bottom drawer of their chest of drawers.[3]

In an attempt to depict the sounds of resurrection, other artists have used the metaphor of singing. Reminiscent of the eternal songs of the angels, the process of what is frozen becoming malleable and what is silent becoming song, is another way of describing the mystery of resurrection. What we observe this side of death is that a person falls silent when they die. Because when they have died we no longer hear their voice, a way of describing resurrection is that their voice is restored not only to speak but to sing.

The image of still figures making sound comes alive in the art of sculpture. The world-famous 'Cantoria', sculpted for the cathedral in Florence by Luca Della Robbia in 1431, is a powerful example of this. Inspired by the timbrels and dances of Psalm 150, Della Robbia created a series of children singing, playing instruments and dancing. Although in reality of course they are silent and still, their stone bodies seem to move and play in an endless dance of joy. Energy pours out from the stone, and when people look at it, they smile. The paradox of living stones is one that we are familiar with from the first letter of Peter. I have to confess that, whenever I have heard that passage (1 Peter 2.4), I have dutifully imagined myself as a square brick, rather like a breeze-block, and that in order to be made into a temple as Peter says, I should support other breeze-block Christians built into solid walls of unassailable faith. Della Robbia's imagination has changed all that for me: the living stones are ones who, like the sculpted children, sing and play and dance even when we are silent and still. These singing stones do shout aloud the exuberant music of Psalm 150, and the children playing the flute call to one another in the marketplace, urging everyone to join the dance (Luke 19.40; 7.32).

When we try to think about death and resurrection and whether there is anything after physical death, we are doing so in a fast-changing, emotional context. Many adults have no direct experience of death until late in life. Thanks to the massive and rapid advances in medical science, and improved nutrition, maternal and infant mortality rates in the West have plummeted. Medical intervention at a time of illness, too, means that fewer of us die from preventable diseases, and so the death of a person, or even attendance at a funeral, is not something many people experience until well into adulthood. There are some individuals whose deaths prompt a public reaction that throws this into sharp relief. Much has been written about the effect on British society of the death of Diana, Princess of Wales, in 1997 as a cultural event as well as a personal tragedy for her family. Pope John Paul II did not hide his own physical deterioration from the public, and the effects of his illness were widely witnessed as he continued to appear on the balcony of his apartment up until his death in 2005. The illness of the reality television star Jade Goody in 2009 brought to public attention the suffering of a young woman facing death too soon, and her funeral drew thousands to the Essex church where she was buried. These very public deaths are sufficiently rare for them to be linked, even though they may have little in common. Jade Goody was described on the day of her death by Stephen Fry as 'Princess Diana from the wrong side of the tracks'. But with the exception of these very public deaths, the truth is that, of the over half a million people who die in the United Kingdom each year, most die in bed, in hospital, hospice or at home in dim light, alone or with one or two others present and out of public view. Unlike in other poorer societies, the number of Britons who die in childbirth or on the battlefield relative to the population is small. The sounds of death are more often the slowing bleeps of the heart machine or the brain monitor or ventilator. It is more likely to be the matter-of-fact tone of the doctor asking her colleagues for agreement as the heart massage is stopped and she looks at her watch to record, 'Time of death . . .' Over three-quarters of British people are cremated, and so the most common experience of dealing with the aftermath of death is no longer that the body is laid out at home for neighbours to pay their respects, but that the closed coffin disappears behind a curtain or is left in the crematorium chapel to the accompaniment of soft music. However it happens, there is a moment, after the medics have left, when the guests from the wake have gone home, when everything is still. Silence falls as the familiar voice is quiet now for ever.

It is into this silence of all silences in John's Gospel, that

Jesus speaks to raise Lazarus – Jesus cries with a loud voice, 'Lazarus, come out.' Unlike the descriptions of Christ's resurrection, this resurrection is a miracle made in the light, with witnesses. This allegorical tale of the new life that Jesus brings is a striking interpretation of resurrection and teaches us not only about ourselves but about God.

Jesus shows deep emotion. He is profoundly moved in his spirit as he approaches the tomb and hears the weeping of Mary and her companions (the same word is used to express the anger of God in Lamentations 2.6), and his emotion is renewed once again as he arrives at the tomb. This is Jesus at his most human, showing grief with which we can identify. He is disturbed, making a noise the Gospel-writers have borrowed from the description of a horse snorting. It is in this seemingly turbulent state that Jesus calls Lazarus forth from the tomb. The word used by the writer of John's Gospel to describe Jesus' loud voice is a rare and old word, κραυγαζω (krow-gad-zo), found only once in the Greek version of the Hebrew Bible and used in both Old and New Testaments to describe the tumultuous sound of a crowd, not the call of one person. In Ezra 3.13 the same word is used to describe the reaction of the people when the foundation of the Temple is laid. It was said that the weeping and joyful singing was so loud that it was not easy to distinguish between the joy and sorrow. Ezra describes a chaotic scene, with the point made several times that the cacophony of crowd sound was all mixed up – the priests and the old people were weeping, but they were also praising the Lord with trumpets. The Levites had cymbals and they sang responsively. It is over all this noise that 'The people shouted so loudly that the sound was heard far away'.

κραυγαζω is the word used just a few verses after the raising of Lazarus in John's Gospel to describe the clamour of the crowd who shout 'Hosanna!' as Jesus rides into Jerusalem on a donkey. It is also the word used to describe the crowd baying for Barabbas and shouting 'Crucify!' (John 19.15).

It is the sound of the crowd at Paul's trial in Acts 22.23 – not just shouting for Paul to be killed, but throwing off their cloaks and tossing dust up into the air. It is a sound of tumult and enormous energy. It is also the shout of the crowd at the arrival of the bridegroom in Jesus' story about the wise and foolish bridesmaids. Everyone is asleep, but at midnight, at an unexpected hour, the shout goes up – 'Here is the bridegroom – come out to meet him!' (Matthew 25.6). It is a shout loud enough to wake not only the sleeping but also the dead.

This is no firm but polite call: it is no gentle invitation that coaxes Lazarus back to life, this is a tumultuous shout to drag Lazarus back from the dead. Jesus screams. We have heard him weep for his friend, we have seen him shudder and snort with fury. Now we hear him scream. These are the sounds made by one who has the power to bring a person back from the dead.

The person of Jesus with which we are presented in this Gospel is inescapably involved with and responsive to the emotions of the people around him. What emerges is an insight that we can allow to take root deep in our spirits: that this side of the mystery of our own resurrection, the call through death to new life sounds like a mixture of 'Hosanna' and 'Crucify!'; that it is not always possible to tell one from the other. We might also reflect that in this life, when we listen for the voice that calls us into freedom, that calls us out of the tombs we construct for ourselves into the light of day, we learn with shocked recognition that it is not always intuitive for human beings to choose to live in the light. We know it's what we should want, and we're taught that it's what we're destined for; but we get a hint of our own unwillingness to accept our vocation to live in the light when we reflect that it's not always straightforward to accept the promise that Christ makes to us that 'I have come that they may have life and have it abundantly' (John 10.10).

George Orwell wrote compellingly of this in relation to the allegory of death and resurrection in the story of Jonah. He speculated on the meaning of Jonah's time inside the belly of the great fish.

> There you are in the dark cushioned space that exactly fits you with yards of blubber between yourself and reality able to keep up an attitude of the completest indifference no matter what happens. A storm that would sink all the battleships in the world would hardly reach you as an echo, even the whale's own movements would probably be imperceptible to you. Short of being dead it's the final unsurpassable stage of irresponsibility.[4]

For Orwell, he was describing what he thought might be a common fantasy. In his interpretation, the belly of the fish was not only an allegorical tomb, but also an adult womb with all its attendant imagery of new life when Jonah was spewed up by the whale. It's a psychological insight into a theological story: the tomb being a place of no responsibility where we are not totally committed to living fully, where we are waiting somehow for real life to begin. Jonah's belly of the fish, the tomb of Lazarus, remind us of our own instincts for safety when we are alarmed by our own potential for living. As adults we often struggle to accept the abundant, extravagant, astonishing life that Jesus offers. As we prepare to face our own fear of the actual and unavoidable journey through our own death and resurrection, we find hints of that fear in our lives now. Through the walls of the tombs we build for ourselves bricked up with low expectations, safe patterns of behaviour that keep us irresponsible, will we hear the roar of God, the shout of Christ's compassion, Christ's exultation mixed with deep anger calling us to live in the light and in the presence of God?

In other resurrection Gospel stories, Jesus, in common with other healers of his day, speaks and touches to raise others from the dead. When Jesus raises Jairus' daughter, he speaks – a command – *talitha cum*. In raising the widow of Nain's son, Jesus speaks again (Luke 7.11ff.). There is in each case a command, a call: the one silenced by death is brought to life by the sound of another. This movement from silence to sound as a depiction of resurrection is captured by Rembrandt in his drawing of St Peter's prayer before the raising of Tabitha. Once again, the resurrection itself is not shown, but the quiet prayer beforehand. It is the moment before the miracle, and Peter, turned away from the dead girl on the bed, is kneeling in front of the window. It is a peaceful scene inside the room, although if we are familiar with the biblical account (Acts 9.36–43), we can still hear the weeping of the widows just the other side of the door. The peace of the scene is underpinned by our knowledge of what is about to happen though. From this stillness, the risk of speaking seems very high, and any moment now, Peter will get up and dare to command a dead girl to live. In this account of resurrection, symbolic of God's call to life in all its abundance, we might recognize this moment of preparation, before we take the risk of speaking from our deepest selves. In praying with Peter in the moment before the miracle, we might learn again that when we are able to say what is in us, others may live. Some years ago I lived for a while in a

L'Arche community. L'Arche is an ecumenical community where adults with learning disabilities live together with assistants sharing life and work day by day. One woman I shared a house with was about five years older than me, with dark hair and big eyes. She spoke just a few words, but she shouted when she was cross and laughed when she was glad, and much of the time she hummed. Her hum was powerful and tuneless, meandering and monotone. One day I was sitting in the garden on the bench with her and she was humming and rocking. We were peaceful, and both seemed contented. After maybe half an hour of meandering humming she momentarily stopped rocking and hummed quite distinctly the tune to 'Mine eyes have seen the coming of the glory of the Lord'. I looked at her and said, 'Hey – do you know what you sang?' We smiled at one another, but in a second the flicker of recognition that had momentarily been there disappeared and she retreated back to where I couldn't reach her. Up to that point and to some extent since, our lives had been absolutely unrecognizable to each other. I don't know what she believed, what she thought of God, or what any of her thoughts were most of the time – she was and is an absolute mystery to me. For that moment, however, despite the chasm fixed between us in some ways, we found a shared language that suddenly I understood. More than that, she created a memory that teaches me about bursting through seemingly impenetrable barriers, and that shows me the mystery of deep connection. Her voice is with me every time I sing the hymn at Easter.

The song of resurrection is the one sung by Stevie Smith's 'Airey Christ' in her poem of the same name. Christ wishes not that people would love him more than anything because he died. Instead, the resurrected Christ – the 'one we had not thought of' – only wishes that people would listen to him sing.

Resurrection is not a metaphor for mere happiness or relief at coming through something difficult. Resurrection is what there is on the other side of nothing. It is the life we had not thought of, and, despite our best efforts, will not be able to imagine.

When Jesus appeared to his disciples behind their locked door, he showed them his wounds and offered them words of peace. It is his wounded body that is raised, not a body restored minus the evidence of his death. The Easter Day resurrection makes no sense without the Good Friday experience. And this crucifixion is carried through the gate of death to the life beyond.

This side of our own death, learning to bear the wounds of grief comes closest to the profound change symbolized by the journey through death to resurrection. In its nihilism and despair, its ability to shut down habitual physical responses, in the fact that there is no way round it, only through it, grief takes us through a combination of exhilaration and despair that consumes us, threatens to overwhelm, and to which there is no certain resolution. When grief visits us suddenly, the noise can be unimaginable, like a car with permanent screeching brakes. When a young girl tripped and fell down the stone steps of her block of flats, she hit her head and died in the ambulance. She was seven. Her family, living high up in an airless flat with brown carpet-tiles and little furniture, used to have the television on all the time. When she died, they couldn't stand the noise but also couldn't bear the unaccustomed silence. I have never been anywhere so quiet as that overcrowded, stunned, grief-stricken flat. Her absence filled the room, yet her father said that he couldn't stop the screaming in his head.

Grief makes us feel crazy, and we hardly recognize ourselves.

A song played randomly on the radio will reduce us to sobbing, so all-consuming that we are disorientated and nauseous and we can't believe we have enough tears to cry it out time after time. After a while, we start to talk to the one who's died: 'It's probably time you came back now, it's enough – you've made your point, just come and say hi. Just walk in and say hello. Let me hear your voice and your laugh and your irritated growl. Anything. Just say hello.' The absence of any reply is oppressively loud until you realize that in fact it has masked all other sounds, and that everything you hear is muffled. Each day you are amazed that the first breath means you are still alive and for a second you are in peace until the noise of missing him or her begins again. Eventually, from the white noise of grief a sadder melody emerges, sometimes almost beautiful again, sometimes almost the song of the singer who has gone. The melody sounds as if it comes from deep within you and is played for you by the resurrected one whose tune it was from the beginning. This is the song of life eternal lived in the present. This is not a logical acceptance of existence after physical death, but a lyrical acceptance that eternity is the context in which we live, the perspective from which we see all creation living and departed. This song of resurrection is only audible after our tight grip on our own mortality is loosened by grief. This can be at the death of one we love, or the death of love itself within a relationship, or an illness that takes us to the edge of our capacity to cope. It is heard by the ones who know the pain of death and bear the wounds of grief. And this song sings of a love that gives dignity to all who sing with it. We are saved from our sin of self-preservation at all costs that separates us from God. We are saved from the mire of mixed motives, selfish ambition and violent competition that disfigures our lives. We are saved from the vacuous over-activity that characterizes a frightened life, and from the temptation born of insecurity to trivialize and dehumanize others.

People who listen for this song of resurrection have also felt the seismic rhythms of grief. They have heard the earthquake of Matthew's Gospel rumble beneath their feet and have known that the stone which they very carefully placed across the path in front of them is no barrier for a Saviour who shouts salvation through the rock. But, we protest, that's my stone: the stone is there to protect me, to shade me, so that I can sit up against it. I need it to be there. It's heavy and looks totally immoveable and gives us a measure of security. The sound of resurrection is for us the same as it was for Mary Magdalene and for Lazarus and for Tabitha. It is our name yelled, whispered, implored by a God who with unimaginable compassion and not a little anger searches and pleads for us to emerge into the light of such love we have never even thought of. Resurrection is of the dead. It is also of the living, and the risk we take, like Abraham and Sarah, like David, Mary, Martha and countless others, is to speak in reply, and for our reply to be yes.

Notes

1. Richard Marsden, 'The Dream of the Rood', *Cambridge Old English Reader*, Cambridge University Press, 2004, p. 192.
2. Geza Vermes, *The Resurrection*, Penguin Books, 2008, p. 6.
3. Quoted in *Stanley Spencer: Letters and Writing*, ed. Adrian Glew, London: Tate Gallery Publishing, 2001, pp. 172, 173.
4. George Orwell, 'Inside the Whale', in *Inside the Whale and Other Essays*, Gollancz, 1940.

CHAPTER 5

The Sound of the Angels

But how alien, alas, at the streets of the city of grief,
where, in the false silence formed of continual uproar,
the figure cast from the mold of emptiness stoutly
swaggers: the gilded noise, the bursting memorial.
Oh how completely an angel would stamp out their
    market of solace,
bounded by the church with its ready-made
    consolations:
clean and disenchanted and shut as a post-office
    on Sunday.[1]

For anyone wanting to attack Christianity, angels are an easy target. The argument goes like this: belief in angels is at best quaint and, at worst, more proof of the infantilizing nature of religious belief. It's all right for children who appreciate that sort of story, but heavenly angels are the product of sentimental religious imaginings that have no place in a world where we have been into space and found that they're not there. They belong to a pre-modern mythology that imagines heaven to be 'up above', full of light and looking remarkably like the court of a human medieval king. The subsections of archangels, seraphim and cherubim are reflections of earthly hierarchies and they are the ultimate proof that Man (and it is men) made

God and his habitation in his own image. To borrow Bertrand Russell's famous comment, we might as well believe in a celestial Teapot that orbits the earth as believe in angels. They make no sense.[2]

For Christians attempting to maintain credibility in a sceptical society, it may seem to be simple common sense to let go of belief in angels as children eventually let go of their belief in fairies or Father Christmas. Christians could consign angels to the 'too difficult' file along with alien abduction, UFO sightings and near-death experiences.

But if we went on such a search for intellectual consistency and social credibility for its own sake, Christians lose more than we gain. The celestial existence and cosmic character of angels have inspired some of the most intense expression in the world's greatest artists. Michelangelo and Leonardo da Vinci painted them, Milton wrote about them, and in fact many ordinary people continue to believe in them. Dying people see them, grieving people are comforted by them. They are characterized as celestial beings that make God a bit more friendly for children, and in a domesticated form they have a hold on people's imagination today. In their popular guise, it's hard not to confuse them with fairies, and for some they represent a kind of post-ghost phase of death.

We are in the realm of myth and metaphor. The very language of straightforward 'Do they or don't they?' is inappropriate here. That's why the question about belief often descends into a sterile assent or denial of the possibility of their existence. So what? There is much confusion about angels, and the definitions and descriptions feel more like a game than a meditation.

I wonder if the key mistake we make about angels is that we try to make ourselves believe in them before we will give any weight to what we know about them. Believing in their existence is not the most fruitful thing we can do with them. No one can prove the existence of angels, and simply asserting that they exist will not further our understanding or deepen our experience of life in the world: listening for them and imagining their presence might. The descriptions of angels in Scripture and the further testimony of people to have seen or heard or felt angels are serious challenges to our imagination. The place of angels in the Christian tradition is an aspect of apophatic theology: the principle that God is absolutely ineffable and beyond the powers of language or description. It is a dead end theologically and personally to focus on whether angels are 'real' or not. They persist in different religions, different centuries and different cultures. The reason that *It's a Wonderful Life* is the favourite film of so many is not because it is a documentary on the principle of making the most of what you have, but an imaginative and emotional exploration of the encounter between a man and an angel that changes the way he lives.

Angels appear throughout Scripture and down the ages in visions of heaven and in descriptions of earth, and our modern Western struggle to imagine meaningful experiences of angels tells us something, not so much about the ridiculousness of angels but about the poverty of our imagination.

Angels live beyond the horizon of what we can possibly understand. We hear whispers of them, see glimmers of them, smell the faint reminiscence of them in the incense of the Church (cf. Revelation 8.4), but as soon as we delineate them, they are gone. Like a celestial version of the children's game Grandmother's Footsteps, where a group of people creep up on a player whose back is turned, it seems that they move when we are not looking, and, when we look hard, they have already disappeared into the wings of the stage or the shadows of a darkened room.

Believing in angels may not be the most important decision we have to make regarding them in order for the tradition to be meaningful for us. To believe is not morally neutral: there have been many belief systems that have brought wickedness into the world. In St Paul's poem celebrating love, he placed hope, faith and love together but gave love the greatest place of honour (1 Corinthians 13). Love is greater than faith; and if you love an angel, that is arguably a more significant gift than believing in him, and you might listen for his song more readily. Perhaps it is not so much believing in them as listening for them that may be closer to a faithful appreciation of them. Angels expose the 'I don't know' of our intellect, but they also capture our hearts so that 'I don't know' is not as easily translated into 'I don't care' as it is when we attempt, for example, the mental gymnastics of the doctrine of the Trinity.

The angels sing. That's what they do. It's what they're for. They also play trumpets and harps, and in Renaissance paintings they recline in the sky, making music for God. In a century where symbols and stories of Christianity are less known than ever before, it is still true that one of the most potent images recognizable to those outside the Christian tradition is that of an angel pictured as a child of Mediterranean extraction with wings and a harp. True to the biblical tradition of the book of Revelation, angels are often shown making music in praise of God in eternity.

Despite our post-Enlightenment scepticism, it is well documented that there have actually been increasing interest in, and sightings of, angels in recent years. It seems that we live in persistently credulous times: we are still attentive to the possibility of their existence. For most people, an angelic experience is something close to a comforting or guarding presence and the inexplicable sense of being accompanied. Cynics will dismiss these experiences as delusional, and some of them may be so. What we do know is that the creatures described as angels in the popular imagination are a domesticated form of the angels of the Christian tradition. Given that angels make music and that this is their purpose and constant activity, we might find a parallel in the cultural development of musical sound that will help us interpret the angelic voice for us today.

The eminent musicologist Anthony Storr has written about the development of music in society and our relationship to it thus:

> Music began as a way of enhancing and co-ordinating group feelings. Today it is often a means of recovering personal feelings from which we have become alienated.[3]

This is a development that is traceable in the accounts of angels in tradition and popular culture. In the Christian tradition, there are innumerable angels worshipping God (Revelation 5.11). This is St John's vision of the essential nature of heaven echoing Isaiah's description: a dynamic flowing, flying eternity that is beautiful, visually dramatic and musically harmonious. The relationships between the angelic host are musical: mutual and just relationships which do not allow for domination or oppression. Each gives way to the other to make the unity (Isaiah 6.3; Revelation 7.11, 12).

As we are in the realm of metaphor, the wonderful descriptions of the loud voices like the sound of many waters (Revelation 19.6), the trumpet calls of the angels in Revelation chapters 8 and 9, the crackling of eternal fire and smoke and the thunderous opening of the Temple (Revelation 11.19) is not to reduce John's vision to one where heaven itself is noisy. (It's not Sydney Smith's description of heaven as eating *paté de foie gras* to the sound of trumpets.)

I can't imagine the music of the angels as a huge celestial brass band, all tubas and trombones. But I can imagine that there is a song that they sing which is more achingly beautiful than I have ever heard: blended, harmonious, evocative, the kind of music that at once reaches in and grasps your heart, making you stare, awestruck, unable to move because to pull away will kill you. It's the kind of thunderous, gentle melody that leaves you struggling to breathe because it has revealed the truth in an instant about love and beauty, loss and restoration. Music that, when you hear it, brings upon you the rush of choking relief that there is, despite your paralysing anxiety, a living and a life beyond the silencing grave. The sounds of the book of Revelation are beyond language and we can feel John of Patmos stretching his imagination as far as he can reach to find words to describe what he hears. He finds sounds such as thunder, earthquake, fire, multitudes of trumpets and voices singing praise and shouting judgement (Revelation 19). This collective experience of angelic music starts with our hearts but won't leave us mired in sentiment. It is the music that binds, and like the blood that flows through a body, it is costly music, poured out to irrigate our earthly unity, bringing it to mutual flowing life.

In popular culture, we have done something quite different with the angels. We have separated them out so that they are no longer in innumerable company but often alone. We talk or sing of an angel, not millions of them. Guardian angels are the most evocative way in which many people encounter the angelic tradition today. Although this personalized protective presence is not one that is developed in Scripture, there are hints of angelic protection.

He will command his angels concerning you to guard you in all your ways. (Psalm 91.11)

Daniel and his companions are saved from death in the lions' den by angels (Daniel 6.22) and angels ministered to Jesus himself in the wilderness (Mark 1.13).

Guardian angels have developed from this biblical tradition into a presence invoked particularly for protection during the hours of darkness. Religious communities invoke still the presence of angels in their nightly prayers at Compline, and as early as the eighth century, liturgies included prayers that God would

. . . send your holy Angel from heaven to guard, cherish, protect, visit and defend all who dwell in this house.[4]

The long religious tradition of guardian angels has developed further in popular culture into a single being that brings not so much protection from harm as escape, diversion, comfort, and usually their message is simply 'Make the most of your life while you can.' Two contemporary examples that have touched millions of people around the world are the song 'Angels' by the British singer Robbie Williams (which is very often requested at funerals in the UK and USA) and 'Angel' which was part of the soundtrack to the 1998 film *City of Angels* and has been a worldwide hit for the Canadian singer Sarah McLachlan.

In each of these songs, sung live to hundreds of thousands of people in concerts and viewed by millions on YouTube and

DVD, the angel is a singular watching presence who will bring comfort in distress. The angel is not so much a harbinger of calamitous truth as in the book of Revelation, but a kind of mothering presence, soothing pain and bringing encouragement. In this way, the song 'Angel' relates to but is not entirely consonant with the film it illustrates. *City of Angels* was itself a re-make of the 1987 German film *Wings of Desire*, and the plots of these films illustrate this movement from an eternal company of strange creatures to a domesticated individual companion. In the German original, a contemporary world is depicted where large numbers of angels move around Berlin, unseen by all except children. In the re-make, this is transferred to Los Angeles. In both films, the angels are all male; they are strong, sexy, unattainable, and the narrative goes that one of them falls in love with a human woman, and makes the choice to leave his eternal world in order to be with her. In his falling to earth he is somehow brought to life as he is able for the first time to feel pain and cry tears and experience loneliness.

Although the 1987 film is more serious and the 1998 re-make lighter, they both imply that romantic love is the catalyst for becoming fully alive, at great cost to the angel who falls. But he never regrets his choice. Human life on earth is better than life in heaven.

Although these developments have moved the popular understanding of angels away from the biblical tradition, Christians shouldn't worry about this. The point is that the currency of angelic presence is still strong in our popular imagination, but these angels don't teach us about God or about eternity or the nature of heaven. They are there as a literary device because imagining them tells us something about life on earth. These modern guardian angels are foils for a set of thoroughly human reflections in the 1987 film about Berlin and its history, and in the 1998 film about loss and love. They are there, not as beings with importance in themselves, but as celestial straight guys for what is essentially a human punchline: romantic love is worth any sacrifice, even life in eternity.

At first glance, this might appear to be not just different from but actually contrary to the Christian tradition and so the use of angels to promote it could provoke a certain amount of Christian indignation. However we interpret these modern angelic myths, the narratives illustrate that we live in a credulous society which wants to – and does – believe in a whole set of things about life that are revealed whether we like it or not.

The Austrian poet Rainer Maria Rilke spent the winter of 1912 alone in a castle at Duino near Trieste. He was evidently restless and heard a voice in the wind: 'Who, if I cried, would hear me among the angelic orders?'[5] His verses, quoted at the beginning of this chapter, illustrate not only the 'false silence of continual uproar' that characterizes modern cities, but the breathtaking nature of angels that we have lost in their current popular domesticated form. Angels as messengers brought news to Sarah and Abraham, deliverance to Daniel, life-changing vocation to Mary, and they heralded the birth of Christ to shepherds in the fields. They were to be found not only in the skies but at the meal table, in places of acute danger, at home and at work. They brought news that was not always comfortable but was decisive and gave direction to those who heard it. 'O how completely an angel would stamp out their market of solace' raged Rilke, dismissing the Church's 'ready-made consolations'. Angels live at the very limits of what we can imagine, and it is to angels we might turn as we listen for the cosmic wisdom that will help us address one of the greatest challenges humans have ever faced: the global ecological crisis of climate change.

While scientists will explore and extend the boundaries of human knowledge about what is happening to the planet and how, people of all faiths have a role in mining their holy texts and their traditions for the wisdom to help us know what to do with what we know. It is the search not only for knowledge but for wisdom that characterizes this exploration, and for Christians the angelic tradition, together with the biblical character of Wisdom, provide signs and symbols that help to give meaning to our new and frightening knowledge. The biblical scholar Margaret Barker, adviser to the Ecumenical Patriarch Bartholomew, has elucidated and developed an inspiring ecological theology rooted in angelic Scripture (particularly the books of Isaiah and Revelation) and other ancient texts such as the first book of Enoch and the Apocalypse of Abraham. She has shown that in the book of Revelation 7.1–8, the picture of the four angels is in harmony with the stunning descriptions of the angels in one of the most important texts for pre-Christian Judaism, and one that influenced the early Church, the first book of Enoch.[6] God regulates the natural elements through the activity of angelic beings (1 Enoch 60.11–22), after sending them out with ropes to measure and bind all that has been made. The angels are ones who bind Creation, sustain its unity, measure its depth and breadth.

According to another, later Jewish text, Adam had heard the song of the angels before he sinned:

> I [Adam] used to hear, before I sinned, the sound of their wings in Paradise, when the seraphim would beat them to the sound of the threefold praise. But after I transgressed, I no longer heard that sound.[7]

Gregory of Nyssa (died 395 CE) opened a Christmas sermon with words from Psalm 118.27 and preached in this vein, that after Adam's and Eve's expulsion from Eden, they were unable to hear the song of the angels. Sin had separated humanity from hearing the liturgy of heaven and it was only at the restoration of the new covenant with the birth of Christ that this was restored. Following Gregory's lead, we might sing our Christmas songs with new meaning. It is at Christmas that the angels make their most vivid appearance in church. The Christmas carol, 'It Came Upon the Midnight Clear', contains the most evocative expression of the restoration of angel song audible on earth as we sing each year, 'O hush the noise ye men of strife and hear the angels sing'.[8] At the birth of Christ, the angels' song has become once again heard on earth. The new covenant is a covenant that reunites earth and heaven, and the character of this covenant is one of a new creation, sung into being by the angels themselves. Heaven and earth are once again reconciled in the coming of Christ, giving us the potential to re-harmonize with the angels who are the invisible bonds of Creation. In post-baptismal anointing rites from the earliest centuries, ears and mouths were anointed, not only to hear and proclaim the word of God, but to be able to listen for the angel song and to join our own voices to theirs.

This teaching that not only are the angels singing the praise of God the Creator but they are the bonds that hold it together is reflected too in one of the apocalyptic Jewish texts written some time after 70 CE, probably around the time that the Christian book of Revelation was being written. In the Apocalypse of Abraham, Abraham is taught to sing by the angel after he has heard the sound of the voice in the fire which is like 'many waters', like 'the voice of the sea in uproar'. Abraham learns the song that the angel sings and is instructed to recite it without ceasing. The angel too sings the song, but Abraham, as a mortal, is required only to join in.[9]

And what is this song that mortals can join, the song of the angels? Margaret Barker, again in her commentary on Isaiah, links the bringing of a just society with the harmony brought by the angels' song. In the Temple tradition, there are three practical components required for a harmonious society: justice, righteousness and peace. Isaiah's vivid picture of the vineyard brings this tradition to life (Isaiah 5.1–7). God plants a vineyard, a creative and ordered environment in which to grow grapes which will make fine wine. The potential of this vineyard is huge, with its stones cleared away and fertile soil, with its hedge and wall and watchtower. It is cultivated earth, in which rich fruit may grow. But the vineyard doesn't flourish:

> The Lord of hosts . . . expected justice but saw bloodshed; righteousness, but heard a cry. (Isaiah 5.7)

If harmony requires justice, peace and righteousness, their counterparts appear in a state of disharmony: bloodshed, a cry of despair and retribution. We might read this parable in English in a straightforward way – the vineyard has failed to produce crops and so will be destroyed. But as Margaret Barker shows, in Hebrew the key words have other meanings insofar as the same sound (or nearly the same sound) means something else and introduces another layer of meaning. For example, she shows that the words for 'grapes' and 'wild grapes' (verse 4) sound very like 'perfume offering' and 'foul smells'. The word for 'hedge' is like the word for 'central shrine'. The word for 'prune' is the same as the word for 'make temple music', the word for 'hoed' is the same sound as 'make glorious'.

So the unpruned and unhoed hedge of the vineyard that was producing sour grapes was also the holy shrine that no longer had the perfumed incense, or the sound of temple music, nor the glory of the Lord. Music and perfume made the holy place 'glorious' and was the sign of righteousness and justice in society.[10]

Further, in Hebrew, the words for 'new' and 'renew' are indistinguishable – and so the often-repeated phrase, 'Sing a new song to the Lord' (e.g. Psalms 96 and 98) is a song of renewal of creation bringing harmony and healing.[11]

If we as human beings are to join in the sounds of the angels, as we are bidden to do, then it is not in sentimental songs about personal guardians who watch over us, however much we might feel comforted by them; it is the song we are taught by the angels of the Christian tradition and one we find in Isaiah's parable of the vineyard – a beautiful and harmonious song of justice, righteousness and peace. It is a song that binds the earth's wounds, that takes seriously the ecology of the created order, that renews and heals. We may as well translate the Lord's Prayer to mean, 'Thy song be sung, on earth as it is in heaven'. These are the ways in which we might re-capture the essence of the scriptural angelic song, and, in dialogue with scientists, cultivate the wisdom that humanity will need to take part in such healing of a fractured world.

The highly respected scientist James Lovelock, himself not a practising Christian although he describes himself as 'marinated in Christian belief',[12] helps us with a contemporary interpretation by giving us a way of imagining the earth as a unified whole. Lovelock is not afraid to use metaphorical language to describe his scientific theories, and so his perspective is widely appreciated by non-scientists as well as his peers.

It is he who appropriated the name of Gaia, the ancient Greek goddess, to describe his imaginative conception of the earth as a whole organism. He has been criticized by Christians over the 40 years of his development of Gaia theory for promoting goddess worship, but that is very far from the truth. His contention is that the earth is itself a whole living organism. It has an almost infinitely complex system of regulatory mechanisms that maintain a stable balance of gases and elements to create a hospitable environment for life. This scientific concept is translated into the poetry of the language of Gaia. He is not suggesting that Gaia actually exists as an entity, but he is offering her name as an appropriate personification for our earth-home that allows us to engage our emotions as well as our intellect. In his book *The Revenge of Gaia* he paints a stark picture of the future: Gaia has a fever (global warming) but we deceive ourselves if we believe that she will not inevitably cool herself down and take revenge on the species who caused her suffering – humans.

> Gaia, the living Earth, is old and not as strong as she was two billion years ago. With breathtaking insolence [humans] have taken the stores of carbon that Gaia buried to keep oxygen at its proper level and burnt them. In doing so, they have usurped Gaia's authority and thwarted her obligation to keep the planet fit for life; they thought only of their own comfort and convenience.[13]

He predicts rapid desertification of the planet and argues that the whole concept of 'sustainable development' is a myth. His historical analogy is that of the invasion of Russia by Napoleon's army in June 1812. Pursuing Tsar Alexander I's army deep into Russian territory, by September two-thirds of the French army had died. This was not from fighting, as the Russian army beat a strategic retreat, but from fatigue, hunger and desertion. Lovelock's warning is that, as a species, human beings have already travelled too far along the path of continuous development and consumption of the earth's resources. Supply lines are thinning, the winter is approaching, and what is needed is not more sustainable development but what he calls 'sustainable retreat'. His warning is that we must soon reduce our activity, consumption and illusion of 'progress' in favour of a return to a life more connected to the earth, less hurried, more simple. He is sceptical of all offsetting strategies either for sustaining our consumption or trying to control it. His argument is that reduction is the only way.[14]

The framing of this warning within the metaphorical person of Gaia is no threat to Christians who are already familiar with the wise and authoritative feminine presence of the scriptural character of Wisdom, 'a tree of life to those who lay hold of her' (Proverbs 3.18). The harmony of the created order visible and invisible is echoed in the figure of Holy Wisdom, who in Proverbs 8 is the one who is present as the Creator God measures and marks out the foundations of the earth and sets the limit of the sea. She is the presence who holds all things together in harmony, like the angels with their invisible cords. We read in Proverbs that this divine feminine presence rejoices in the inhabited world and delights in humanity. It is the right use of knowledge, the wise application of what we know, that brings harmony (Proverbs 8.32). The apocryphal book of the Wisdom of Solomon describes Holy Wisdom in similar terms:

Though she is but one, she can do all things, and while remaining in herself, she renews all things; in every generation she passes into holy souls and makes them friends of God, and prophets. (Wisdom of Solomon 7.27)

Throughout the Christian tradition, there have been wise and authoritative women who have articulated a Christian understanding of creation. The seventh-century abbesses Hilda of Whitby, whose patronage fostered the poet Caedmon and whose spirituality under the influence of Aidan was steeped in the Celtic rootedness in the land, and Ethelburga, presiding over her Benedictine agrarian community at Barking; the twelfth-century abbess and musician Hildegard of Bingen and the fourteenth-century mystic Mother Julian of Norwich. These wise and authoritative feminine presences are inheritors of the Wisdom tradition: one which takes seriously the beauty of the earth, listens to its lessons and interprets them for the communities of their day in such a way that men and women looked to them for leadership and truth. Although the Gaia principle has been appropriated by New Age spiritualities, much to the regret of Lovelock himself, it is a sensibility with which Christians might be more comfortable, following the scriptural tradition of Holy Wisdom, of which Jesus himself was the ultimate example.

In order to join the song of the angels as heard by Isaiah and John of Patmos and the shepherds in the fields, we are asked to listen for these angelic songs in our communities, in the songs of the earth, in our human institutions. The contemporary American theologian Walter Wink has found a language in which to express to a modern audience the complexities of the book of Revelation which addresses its instructions not to the people but to 'the angels of the churches' (cf. Revelation 2.1). Rather than imagining separate creatures that fly in the sky, a characterization which marginalizes angelic presence and power, his contention is that any institution – a church, a social club, a company, a sports club or a nation – has an enduring spirit that is discernible over generations and doesn't seem to be dependent on the particular people who inhabit that institution at any one time.[15] This imaginative interaction with the ancient tradition of Revelation emphasizes the connection rather than the distance between humanity and angels. He argues for an integral world-view that takes seriously the ancient understanding that everything on earth has a heavenly counterpart and our prayers are 'matched by prayer by the angels in heaven'.[16] But it is a world-view that makes prayer central because, even after the insights of science have been taken into account, 'the spiritual is at the core of everything and infinitely permeable to prayer'. This integrated world-view is one that emphasizes our connection to the whole of creation, in the tradition of the angels.

It is an angel that saves Shadrach, Meshach and Abednego from the fiery furnace in Daniel, and it is the apocryphal song of praise that they sing to God from the furnace that forms the *Benedicite*, the canticle of Creation that is said or sung in religious communities and Christian churches at Morning Prayer all over the world. A key feature of this canticle is that it is not until halfway through the song that anything living begins to sing. Within the context of the angels' song (the first to sing God's praise), it is the waters, the sun and moon, the stars, the rocks, ice and snow that praise God until the whales, the fowls of the air, the beasts and cattle begin to sing too. This integrated ancient expression of the Gaia principle brings us full circle as we note that, in the Christian and Jewish traditions, the angels sing praise to the Creator, and in doing so, they, with Holy Wisdom, bind and heal the created order.

For Christians, the sounds of the angels on earth that we

join are those instincts to worship, to give value to something greater and more profound than ourselves that sing for peace and justice and that long for the unity of the whole creation. They are also songs that warn of approaching cataclysm (Revelation 8.8–13), and in acknowledging our own place within the created order, imagining the song of the angels saves us from arrogance. Angels are an antidote to religious or scientific reductionism because their persistence in our imagination is inexplicable. They remain stubbornly other, elusive but present, and their scriptural testimony challenges a modern Western way of life that is causing so much damage to the planet's balance. It is a perspective that we wilfully ignore at our peril. It is not surprising that we have attempted to domesticate them so that they become our servants, whose function is simply to comfort us in our personal trauma.

A Jesuit astronomer told me the story of the setting up of the Kitt Peak National Observatory in Arizona in the United States. The chosen site for the observatory, based on its clear skies, was within the Papago Indian reservation, and so permission was sought from the Tribal Council to begin tests to see if it was indeed a suitable site for an observatory. The lease was signed in 1958 and because there was no word in the Papago language for 'astronomer', the translation read 'the people with long eyes'.

It was the twentieth-century Anglican priest Austin Farrar who likened the Church to a telescope, whose purpose was to scan the heights and depths of creation always looking for God.[17] In this way, perhaps Christians are asked to be people with long eyes, who, like astronomers, are willing to wait, often in the cold and darkness, whose desire is to contemplate and experience the wonders and mysteries of the universe. Inasmuch as a telescope is a way of receiving and translating light through a series of lenses in order that the unfathomable universe, ever expanding and accelerating, is observable by human beings, the Church too can be a community of people who listen together for the unfathomable songs of eternity sung in praise to the Creator by the created, led by the angels. In this contemplative listening, the Church translates the song and teaches it to others so that we become more than observers, and participators in the music of the cosmos. Bringing the heavens into focus is not just a visual task; and we know that the mystery of the universe is contained in one cell of our bodies as much as in the furthest-flung star. As our scientific knowledge of the earth's processes grows, we know that deforestation, increasing rates of extinction, melting of the ice-caps and the destruction of the ozone layer are damaging the balance of the ecosystems of which we are part and on which we depend. In the damage done to our planet, we hear the warnings of the angels who praise their Creator ceaselessly and who long for us to participate in their work of binding and healing this wounded earth.

Notes

1. Rainer Maria Rilke, 'Tenth Duino Elegy', quoted in Neil Astley (ed.), *Staying Alive*, Bloodaxe Books, 2002, p. 44.
2. Bertrand Russell, in his commissioned but not published article in 1952 for *Illustrated* magazine.
3. Anthony Storr, *Music and the Mind*, HarperCollins, 1992, p. 122.
4. 'Gelasian Sacramentary' (eighth century), quoted in Michael McMullen (ed.), *Clouds of Heaven*, SPCK, 1999.
5. Astley, *Staying Alive*, p. 30.
6. Margaret Barker, *The Great High Priest*, T. & T. Clark, 2003, p. 111.
7. 'Testament of Adam', 1.4, a Jewish text from perhaps second century CE, taken over by the Church.
8. Margaret Barker, Temple Studios Group Symposium, May 2009. *Temple Music: Meaning and Influence*: see www.templestudiesgroup.com.

9. *The Apocalypse of Abraham*, chapter 17, verses 4–6.
10. Conversation with Margaret Barker, 5 December 2008.
11. Margaret Barker, in a paper given to the Temple Studies Group, May 2009; www.templestudiesgroup.com.
12. James Lovelock, *The Revenge of Gaia*, Penguin, 2006, p. 137.
13. Lovelock, *The Revenge of Gaia*, p. 146.
14. Lovelock, *The Revenge of Gaia*, p. 149.
15. Walter Wink, *The Powers That Be*, Doubleday, Augsburg Fortress, 1998.
16. Wink, *The Powers That Be*, p. 184.
17. Sermon preached by Austin Farrar, Pusey House, Oxford, 1960, in Austin Farrar, *The End of Man*, SPCK, 1973, p. 52.

CHAPTER 6

Our Sound is Our Wound

In the biblical accounts of Jesus' resurrection appearances, it is Thomas who wants to touch his wounds. Thomas, who along with the others has followed Jesus for years, who has watched in horror as the dream seemingly came to an end with his arrest and execution, who is afraid, living behind locked doors, is understandably sceptical when his companions tell him they've seen Jesus alive. Thomas, absent from the group at the crucial moment, now wants to convince himself that the miraculous might be possible.

> Unless I see the mark of the nails in his hands, and put my finger in the mark of the nails and my hand in his side, I will not believe. (John 20.25)

A week later, Jesus appears again among his disciples and invites Thomas to do just that. In the end, despite the memorable artistic depictions of Thomas with his hand in Jesus' side, we don't read in Scripture that he does touch him: he simply says to Jesus, 'My Lord and my God.' Jesus seems to rebuke him as he tells him that those who have not seen and still believe are the ones who are blessed.

When we call ourselves witnesses to an event, it is usually the testimony of our eyes that counts. Somehow above the other senses, we attribute more value to the information provided by our eyes. The admission that 'I must have misheard' is common. We never say that we have mis-seen. Our other senses – taste, smell, touch – are even less authoritative. This informal hierarchy of senses has implications for a theology attentive to people with disabilities, but it is worth noting that, in this story, Jesus' words challenge our assumptions, giving honour to those who 'have not seen and yet believe'.

This book is an attempt to be a witness to the sounds that we make as a society, and as a body of people called out of humanity to follow Christ.

There are those in our cacophonous society (led by the ones who have been dubbed the New Atheists) who are beginning to say more aggressively that the sounds of public religion should be silenced, that religious observance is essentially personal and should remain exclusively private, and does not warrant a place in the public square. This manifests itself not only in objections to bishops sitting by right in the House of Lords, but in the hostility with which comment from faith leaders on subjects of public interest is greeted. Debate polarizes quickly on religious practice in schools (as opposed to the teaching of comparative religion) and issues of medical ethics such as assisted dying or abortion and from time to time broader questions about the direction of society.

Christianity has itself travelled some way in its relationship with those who exercise political and economic power. From a fledgling movement in hiding and under persecution from political and religious authorities which operated behind locked doors and with secret signs, an emperor was converted and the world changed. European political and religious leadership eventually became conflated. In England, for example, the Lord Chancellor was almost always a bishop for medieval monarchs until Henry VIII dismissed Cardinal Wolsey; and the last bishop to hold high financial office (as Lord Treasurer) was William Juxon, Bishop of London in the 1630s. The last bishop to hold any high political office was John Robinson, Lord Privy Seal under Queen Anne in the first years of the eighteenth century. In contrast, today leaders of the established Church speak on matters of policy from the perspective of critical friend rather than government minister. This voice is mediated to society at large, as in the case of any area of public life, by radio, television and the internet. Comment by individuals is reported, but public prayer is heard less and less as market-driven audience figures determine the dominant sounds that we hear in the public square.

Compare, for example, the sound of religion with the sound of the quasi-religion – football – mediated to the public in an average winter week in Britain. Now that referees wear microphones, a huge variety of sounds is associated with the game. During the hours of broadcast games, the shouting of the players to one another on the pitch combines with the voice of authority from the referee; the excitement of the commentator and the swelling chants of the crowd; the fury of the manager in the post-match interview over the penalty he thought was unfair; and the chatty analysis of pundits in the studio. Not only this, but on 24-hour channels every news bulletin has a sports update. There isn't a special section at the end of news broadcasts, for example, for new musical compositions released that day, or a 'health update' or 'science news'. The areas of human activity that are given prominence in a special section every half-hour are sport, business and the weather. The reality is that in London, more people attend a Christian church on Sunday than attend a football match on Saturday; but these numbers of people – not just people who express a vague interest but who actually get out of their houses for 90 minutes of collective experience – are nothing when compared with the eye-watering figures involved in television deals for football clubs. Can you imagine the interest and hours given to football being transferred to the people and activities of the modern Church of England for example? Instead of a couple of hours given to broadcasting services on the national networks BBC Radios Three and Four, there would be hours of weekly worship broadcast from around the country; the appointment of a bishop would make headlines because of 'the surprise move from Norwich to Manchester'; and the transfer market would lead to speculative interviews with churchwardens immediately after their Sunday service denying the interest shown in their vicar from another parish.

It's not an analogy that bears sustained scrutiny, and I won't linger long on the relative elements of competitiveness and staged conflict that each activity displays, but in listening to the sound of each, particularly as portrayed on television, internet and radio, there are some similarities – the collective singing, the co-ordinated physical movement of a crowd (clapping or sitting or standing) and the faithful commitment of thousands. In its portrayal on television, football is noisy, blokey (even when presented by women), physical, feverish at times and often highly emotional. The Church's sound in comparison seems much less heartfelt, by turns nonchalant or shrill, still predominantly masculine but in a different way, less fervent and a little distracted. To use an economic term, society simply has more invested socially, emotionally and financially in the web of relationships that make up the football industry and so it makes more noise.

Public religious observance depends not only on words but

on symbolic sounds. The argument that religion does not deserve a place in the public square depends on the postmodern reflection that individuals believe a whole set of things not expressible in the communal doctrines imposed by an authoritative religion. To an extent this is true, and has always been so. It is true that private, intimate belief is largely unspoken, and in any given congregation of people who have gathered to worship, there will be a great variety of convictions, some of which will not relate to the public articulation of that faith. Many people who attend a Christian funeral will believe in their heart of hearts that reincarnation is a serious possibility, others believe deep down that despite what the Church says publicly in its funeral rites, there probably isn't really any existence after we die. But symbolic sounds are often more powerful than any set of words.

For example, two weeks after the bombings in central London of July 2005, the Mayor declared that at midday there would be two minutes' silence. At St Paul's Cathedral, a bell was tolled in the minutes leading up to 12 noon. Cars pulled over, taxis and buses stopped their crawl up Ludgate Hill, and thousands of office workers poured out of the buildings and began to gravitate towards the cathedral. The bell was a public sound onto which each person presumably projected his or her own thoughts and feelings. Some were personally sad as it reminded them of their mother's funeral; others were something akin to nervous as they remembered they had not yet had the courage to take the Tube since it happened; some were defiant, reclaiming the streets from terrorists who killed people so randomly; some were simply moved by the huge and respectful crowds who packed Fleet Street and Cheapside. In a public act of commemoration, the ancient sound of the tolling bell called thoroughly modern city workers away from their bleeping computers and vibrating mobiles to stand in silence before breaking up into groups as they walked to an early lunch and talked over what had happened.

The Christian Church has an historic role expressed in this story – to call people into silence in the presence of God. It is a role that has particular meaning at a time of tragedy, but, given society's increasing noise, has more contemporary urgency and focus in today's world. To fulfil this role, the churches must practise silence in order to create something for others to join.

Much is written (and ironically said) about intentional silence in the Church. Not much is said about it in society, unless it is the second week in November, and then it's usually a quirky cultural reflection on the place of silence in the act of remembering. A minute's absence of noise is a regular feature of large crowds gathering at the start of rugby or football matches, always in recognition of a death or of the anniversary of a death. But silence is one distinctive contribution the churches can make in a noisy society, after the example of Christ, who often retreated to the mountains to pray at night alone.

One of the best-loved descriptions of God in Scripture, popularized in the well-known hymn, is the 'still, small voice', more recently translated as 'the sound of sheer silence' (1 Kings 19.12). God was not in the earthquake, nor in the fire or the wind, but God was to be found in the still, small voice. We still struggle to listen for that voice in an over-busy church in an over-busy world where those of us who lead services let our congregations down whenever we say 'Let us keep silence' and then keep talking. It is a modern (and perhaps also not so modern) phenomenon that when we church people talk about silence, we are often expressing not so much a deep yearning for stillness in which we may commune with God, as a distaste for vulgar noise and a desire for peace and quiet in the same way as the Victorian rector retreated into the study when the children played too loudly. We often don't mean silence, we mean the right kind of noise. In a world of constant noise, church communities can teach themselves to be oases of stillness, witnessing to a different reality, one that doesn't need endless distraction and clamour to communicate it.

The reality is that we often replicate rather than challenge life in a noisy world. Because of this, collective silence in church services can cause immense anxiety. For parents, it is certain that as soon as the person at the front introduces a moment of quiet, their children will begin to cry and they will feel not only the anxiety of the effort required trying to keep children quiet, but the judgement of others. For older people who live alone, it may be that more silence is the last thing they need, and the collective silence of a congregation reminds them of their own too-quiet home. Silence doesn't just happen, and it takes a long time for groups to be comfortable with it.

As we explore the theme of silence in our lives, it's a pertinent challenge for any person of faith to keep a sound diary just as those wanting to lose weight keep a food diary. What are the sounds you hear in a day? How much do you hear, and what do you feel about that? How much music is in your life, and what kind of music is it? Is there any silence? How do you feel when there is? What sounds are going on inside your head? Are there snatches of conversation or bits of tune, are there inexplicable or unidentifiable noises or is there nothing? Are any of these sounds related to your physical aural environment?

All of this is relevant for people of faith who want to find ways to listen for the presence of God, not in terms of hearing physical voices but in the discipline of discernment, a desire to align our will with the will of God. Learning about our attitudes to noise and silence will assist in our attempts to become and remain attentive to the presence and will of God deep within us. Cultivating an inner silence will require nurture, attention, care.

One theme underlying much of the reflection in this book has been that silence is not in itself neutral. The silence of the silenced, the silence of the unmarked graves of the disappeared, is Hildegard's satanic silence, the silence of the fallen angels, a stultifying silence with which the body of Christ should never be complicit. A shared silence, such as that of the Quaker meeting or the purposeful remembering of people who have died, or such as the contented silence of long-time companions who don't need to make conversation, is a different proposition. A silence that is underpinned by love, by a willingness to wait, by a level of attentiveness that accepts where we are and who we are now before God, is a gift that the churches can give to such a distracted world.

The churches' wounds are on display when we are unable to be silent or to invite others into such a silence. But sometimes, with the ancient sounds of bells and evocative music, we can do so. On the anniversary of 9/11 it has become a tradition that London clergy visit one of the firms that lost many colleagues in the twin towers tragedy of 2001. Each year, on 11 September, the current traders give their profits to children's charities and clergy have led prayers as the day begins. Recently we have taken choristers aged between eight and thirteen along with us.

At 8.30 a.m. on the large open-plan trading floor, the day was in full swing. About a hundred men – and they were all men – in their 20s and early 30s sat at long desks with computer screens in front of them, shouting into their phones. As a picture of modern capitalism, it was a compelling scene. Insofar as a large group of people were all performing the same task in a noisy environment, the room looked like the twenty-first-century version of the factories of the Industrial Revolution: a place where prayer, music and silence could not be further from the minds of those working there. As the suited man leapt up to introduce us over the microphone, he said, 'Let business continue – let's keep making the money', giving the traders permission to carry on trading through the prayers. And the choristers began to sing over, or was it under the noise, *Dona Nobis Pacem*. The ancient languages of Latin and chanted melody sung by children brought a timeless message of peace which jarred against the fast-paced aggression of the business of increasing profit.

But they persisted, and gradually the shouting became a little subdued: not only did the traders talk more quietly, but they began to stop and listen. As the beautiful singing continued, some started to hold up their phones so that the office on the other side of the world could hear the song, and by the time the last *Dona Nobis Pacem* was sung, there was indeed a measure of peace.

In a society where the majority of people live their lives without reference to organized religion, the language and message of the Church are as counter-intuitive as a group of children singing about peace on a trading floor. But it is into this shouting society that a travelling preacher walks, ready to sing words of peace, ready to wash the feet that are weary from pounding the treadmill of getting and selling. His own feet have been washed and anointed by the woman who treads tenderly beside him – the woman who is herself a sinner, forgiven, from the city (cf. Luke 7.36ff.).

On the eve of the G20 summit in March 2009, the Prime Minister suggested that shared global values were needed in order to build regulation into the future of the world's markets. In attempting to articulate these values, he quoted what is often called the Golden Rule: 'Do to others as you would have them do to you.' It is true that Jesus quoted this well-known saying, and it is a precept that Christians share with other world religions. But as one twentieth-century theologian pointed out as he attempted to draw political conclusions from the life of Jesus, the distinctive teaching of Jesus is not only 'Do to others as you would have them do to you', but more directly, 'Do as I have done to you.'[1] There is a distinction to be drawn between mimicking Jesus and following him.[2] New Testament teaching does not lead us to live precisely the *same* life as Jesus: that of an unmarried male carpenter. We are not called to *be* him, but to be ourselves and *follow* him. This will mean embodying the nature of God's love as revealed by Christ on the cross:

> The concrete social meaning of the cross is in its relation to enmity and power. Servanthood replaces dominion, forgiveness absorbs hostility.[3]

Following Jesus as a disciple will mean as many different journeys as there are people. There is much to interpret and much to discuss. Translated into our context of sound, we are not called to mimic Jesus as an impressionist would, but we are called to echo Christ's voice and imitate his silence.

Of course it's true that the actions and motives of the historical Jesus of Nazareth are impossible to verify in detail, and in flat description the biblical texts leave more questions than they answer. We should not base a whole theological perspective on the choice of one or two Greek verbs, but when the voice of Christ is set in the context of the voices throughout Hebrew and Christian Scripture, then its resonance is constantly provoking, startling and revealing of the nature of God. Christ shudders with anger, snorts, shouts, and the visceral nature of this compassion teaches us not only about what God is like, but about what it could be like to be human.

Where would Christ's voice be heard, for example, in the ubiquitous and influential daytime television programmes that expose private family situations to the public glare? The rise and rise of these shows, becoming ever more extreme in the constant attempt to win bigger audiences, is a symptom of a society shrill with moral confusion at a loss for where to turn for guidance and wisdom. Ironically, for religion is never mentioned on these programmes, never better has Jesus' prediction that 'what is whispered in private will be shouted from the rooftops' been brought to life for a global audience.

A series of groups of people, all with similar factual circumstances ('My girlfriend slept with my best friend and now I don't know if her baby is mine') explores their own situations in front of a studio audience, and with the goading of a host, who varies from 'honest broker' to 'the voice of reason', the complexity of each particular set of relationships is exposed and picked over. The motivation of the very vocal audience is often the focus of public criticism – 'a human form of bear baiting' one judge commented.[4] The crowd are not any different from us; the inheritors of the ones who knitted as the guillotine fell during the French Revolution; who turned up to Smithfield to watch a hanging; who now crowd around the van crawling through the security gates at the Old Bailey; the ones who would witness a public crucifixion. These shows are immensely popular. In 2007, in competition with all the hundreds of available channels, one show was quoted as regularly attracting a third of all viewers watching television at that time (*The Jeremy Kyle Show*).[5]

The motivation of the participants is less clear. A need to explain, to find out the truth, a desire to purge oneself or blame another, are all thoroughly understandable human desires, but to explore this in public, with the baying crowd as part of the cast, distorts the issues, and participants have publicly said they regret taking part. The dynamic between host, contributor and audience is a cross between public confession and public punishment. Unlike the stocks where the victim is silent, the tone of both participants and audience varies from strident to aggressive, self-justifying to defensive; sometimes contrite and occasionally conciliatory. The potent combination of defiance and shame when patterns of circumstances, addictive or abusive behaviour, are exposed to the viewing public, intoxicates us, and it seems we can't tear ourselves away. A proper self-acceptance is, in front of an audience, translated into a jaw-jutting 'Take it or leave it – this is who I am.'

In watching these shows, I am often reminded of the sanctimonious crowd who flung the woman caught 'in the very act of committing adultery' at Jesus and demanded that he do something about it (John 8.1–11). In John's Gospel it is a busy, fussy scene full of outraged religious types followed by a judgemental crowd. In reaction to their demands, Jesus does not pronounce judgement. He pauses and silently crouches down to write on the ground before expressing immense compassion for this vulnerable, dishevelled woman dragged from the arms of the man she shouldn't have been with. He does speak, but speaks words of compassion and understanding into the furious condemnatory tones of her accusers. From the silence of his first reaction, he then refuses to condemn her and sends her on her way with words of encouragement for her to lead a better life: 'and from now on do not sin again'. The audiences and participants, not to mention the counsellors and security guards who work on these shows, would each have a very different definition of what might constitute sin in the variety of situations paraded in front of the crowd. Many would reject the concept of sin completely. In relation to this, the churches listen for the echo of the voice of Christ that is not afraid to be silent until there is something to say, even when the crowd bays for a quick answer. The churches' voice echoes the voice of Christ who speaks peace, forgiveness and transformation into the complex circumstances of human relationships. And while championing accountability, and while not colluding with secrecy, churches should not be afraid, like Christ, to send the crowd away with a challenge, to be left alone quietly with the ones feeling humiliated and love them into healing and change, finding a way, too, to wash their feet.

These shows are the sounds of a society where individual complexities are fetishized and the unending hunt continues for someone to blame. They reveal wounds born of insecurity in our own identity, they reveal a wound of fear of death and a tendency to self-harm.

The character of the Christian vocation emerges in the midst of this hurting world. Are we a body of people whose instinct is to fall into the silence of waiting on God with a willingness to listen with our whole bodies for the presence of the Holy One we will recognize in that sound of sheer silence?

Are we a body of people who know in our own lives the value of silence in a noisy world and teach this to our children and grandchildren? Are we a body of people at peace with our own death? Are we a body of people whose visceral compassion for a suffering world is expressed in our actions, our words, and the tone of our voice?

Are we a body of people who know the language and music of lament, who have learned how to sing out our own pain? Are we a body of people whose worship of God is in tune with the songs of the angels rooted in the groans of the earth?

Jesus of Nazareth lamented for the suffering of the world and shuddered with compassion for all who suffered distress and exclusion. He cried with a loud voice to bring others new life, did not remain silent in the midst of torture, and is forever in the presence of the music of the angels in eternity.

The Church is the body of Christ on earth. What would it mean for this body to weep with Rachel for the lost children who are soldiers and prostitutes, sweatshop workers and exploited consumers, to lament with Jesus over the city that never sleeps? How can the Church scream with Christ to summon life from death, and insist on speaking in the face of persecution of all in danger?

The seventeenth-century priest and poet John Donne (1572–1631) described the Church itself as an echo of the voice of God:

> The scriptures are God's voice, the church is His echo – a re-doubling, a repeating of some particular syllables and accents of the same voice.[6]

For the Church to re-double and repeat the accent of God's voice, our starting point has to be deep attentiveness to Scripture as it is proclaimed and lived, and a commitment to search for the silence Jesus needed so often. From this attentive inner silence we are able to speak, catching the echo of the voice of God as we have heard it from the beginning. There is a cost to speaking with this accent, as it will associate us, as Peter's did on the night of Jesus' arrest, with the one crucified by frightened and violent men (Matthew 26.73). We will often confront, as Peter did, our own capacity for betrayal and cowardice. But when, like Peter, we have heard Christ's words of restoration, we will, from our greatest failure and deepest fear, acknowledge our need for forgiveness and help to change the world.

The character Emmanuel Nene puts this succinctly in Alan Paton's novel *Ah But Your Land is Beautiful*:

> Don't worry about the wounds. When I go up there which is my intention, the big judge will say to me 'Where are your wounds?' And if I say I haven't any, he will say 'Was there nothing to fight for?'[7]

As we choose our battles and listen for the songs of lament and freedom in a world bellowing with violence and fear, we live our lives attentive to the movement of the Spirit and know that it is in the love of God that we find rest from a noisy world.

> If I speak in the tongues of mortals and of angels but do not have love I am a noisy gong or a clanging cymbal. (1 Corinthians 13.1)

Living our lives grounded in this love will leave us wounded, but will cultivate our compassion. This love will nurture our courage and help us find our voice. This love will seize our hope and insist on justice. And the sound of this love is God's redemption song that, when we have heard it, we too long to sing.

Notes

1. John Howard Yoder, *The Politics of Jesus,* Wm B. Eerdmans, 1972, p. 119.
2. Yoder, *The Politics of Jesus,* p. 120.
3. Yoder, *The Politics of Jesus,* p. 130.
4. Alan Berg, *The Guardian,* 24 September 2007.
5. *The Guardian,* 24 September 2007.
6. Sermon 6.217 from *The Sermons of John Donne,* ed. Evelyn M. Simpson and George R. Potter, University of California Press, 1962.
7. Alan Paton, *Ah But Your Land is Beautiful,* Scribner Paperback Fiction, 1981.

Acknowledgements

I owe enormous thanks to many people who have taken the time to discuss ideas, share their stories and support the writing of this book. Without the wise guidance of Cecilia and Bryan Winkett, Patrick Craig, Susan Knowles and Carole Irwin, the draft would never have become a text. I am hugely grateful to Caroline Chartres whose enthusiasm and belief were infectious and never allowed me to think I wouldn't finish this first attempt at a book. My colleagues at St Paul's carried me through the improbable combination of taking part in Holy Week liturgies and correcting drafts, and their interest and support have been unfailing. I am especially grateful to the people who allowed me to use their stories in this book. Without their inspiration I would not have been able to find my voice: they know who they are and I thank them profoundly. I also thank Archbishop Rowan, whose prayerful leadership teaches me about God. Mistakes and omissions are mine for which I take full responsibility, and in writing these lines I am aware that, while one name is affixed to the title, authorship is a shared endeavour born from my life lived in community.

Index

Index

Index